The Balanced Way to Cook

Gourmet

A GIFT OF HEALTH

The Balanced Way to Cook
Gourmet

A   GIFT   OF   HEALTH

The Women's Leadership Group of the Boys & Girls Clubs of Greater Washington is a dynamic force of influential women who give generously of their time, talents, and resources to help improve the lives of kids in the greater Washington area. *The Balanced Way to Cook Gourmet* is a project of the Women's Leadership Group to benefit the Boys & Girls Clubs of Greater Washington.

Copyright 2003 by Boys & Girls Clubs of Greater Washington
8555 16th Street, Suite 400
Silver Spring, Maryland 20910
301.562.2000

Library of Congress Number: 2003109068
ISBN: 0-9729853-0-1

Designed and Manufactured by Favorite Recipes® Press, an imprint of

FRP

P.O. Box 305142, Nashville, Tennessee 37230
800.358.0560

AUTHOR/EDITOR: Patti Sowalsky
PUBLISHING DIRECTOR: Patty Perkins Andringa
MARKETING DIRECTOR: Andrea Fraser-Reid Farr
PHOTOGRAPHY: Ed Whitman, Lightstruck Studio
FOOD STYLIST: Robin Lutz
BOOK DESIGN: Sheri Ferguson Kimbrough

Manufactured in the United States of America
First Printing: 2003   19,000 copies
Recipe for the cover photo on page 70.

Preface

Over the years many things have changed but one
thing remains true: children always need a safe place to go
and grow. Boys & Girls Clubs of Greater Washington has been
that place for over a century. By passing through the doors
of twenty-seven Boys & Girls Clubs and four Group Homes in
the Greater Washington area, 35,000 children are safe,
encouraged, valued, and loved.

Between the hours of 3:00 P.M. and 8:00 P.M. every day,
children participate in programming that encourages young
people to engage in positive behaviors that nurture their
well-being and teach them to set personal goals and live
successfully as self-sufficient adults.

Just as Boys & Girls Clubs strives to keep kids healthy,
The Balanced Way to Cook Gourmet offers cooking solutions
to keep them and you healthy. Support The Positive Place For
Kids. Buy this Gift of Health and, at the same time, you will
be supporting the Boys & Girls Clubs of Greater Washington.

Contents

Introduction

Have you ever stared longingly at a slice of Key lime pie but thought it might literally be too rich for your blood? Look no further! The recipes in this cookbook are designed specifically to teach techniques that will allow you to cut down on the fats and carbohydrates in your diet so that you will be able to have your favorite "goodies" without costing you your health!

In addition to an in-depth explanation of facts about both fats and carbohydrates, this cookbook is designed to let you continue to still enjoy, with some modifications, many of the foods you love. Each recipe is one that has been scrutinized and adjusted to remove or lower some of its potentially harmful saturated fat and refined carbohydrate content without sacrificing aroma, texture, or appeal. It is a cookbook that emphasizes the importance of the moderation and balance that need to be maintained between various food groups in order to maintain good health and nutrition.

Did you know that by eating prepared and fast foods, Americans are on a sugar high because they are ingesting an average of thirty-two teaspoons (or 128 grams) of refined sugar daily, far above the safe and recommended average of six to twelve teaspoons? Much of this granulated refined sugar, the number one additive in the American food supply, is corn-based fructose which is SIX TIMES sweeter than regular sugar. Consumed in such large amounts, it wreaks havoc on our insulin levels and has caused an EPIDEMIC of type II diabetes, especially among our children, who would rather drink a glass of heavily promoted fructose-laden soda than a glass of milk. It is also a major cause of heart disease because the body stores excess sugars as triglycerides, fats that elevate the LDL, or "bad," cholesterol levels in our bodies. The combination of large portions of processed and fast foods containing sugar, salt, saturated fat, and starch additives, together with our sedentary lifestyle, has caused us to become obese at such an alarming rate that the medical community is witnessing an obesity health crisis.

Taking the easy way out by constantly relying on fast and prepared food, sold to us in ever increasing and excessive portions, is taking its toll on the health of Americans. We MUST educate ourselves about what we choose to eat so that we can avoid consuming unnecessary additives and excessive calories. To accomplish this and to know what we are putting in our bodies, we MUST make an effort not just to GET BACK TO COOKING, but to get back to a NEW WAY OF COOKING!

In *The Balanced Way to Cook Gourmet,* you will find: what and why certain foods are more ideal to eat than others; what combinations make a meal well balanced; how to make recipe substitutions that reduce or eliminate unnecessary saturated fats and sugars; and more. All of the delicious and easy-to-make multicultural recipes in this book are accompanied by notes that not only detail often surprising food facts but also suggest where some of the more unusual ingredients might be purchased. In addition to hints about cooking techniques, there are others that address cooking equipment and its care. By using this book you will, with little effort, get into cooking. Consider it a sport, or a creative artistic venture, or a hobby. But most of all, consider it a Gift of Health to you and your family.

Nutrition
IN A NUTSHELL

WHAT YOU SHOULD KNOW
ABOUT WHAT YOU EAT

When it comes to cooking and eating, we Americans are seriously off balance. We cook TOO little, and we eat far TOO much fast and prepared foods in quantities that are simply TOO large for our own good. We believe that if a product's package boasts, in bold letters, that it is fat free or contains no cholesterol, it must be good or healthy for us. Rarely do we look beyond this "headline" to assess the product information that, by law, is listed on each packaged food item. Many of us turn a blind eye when it comes to informing ourselves about food facts, because it has become easier and faster to buy prepared products or fast food than it is to cook from scratch. We pay no attention to the fact that the ingredients that manufacturers commonly manipulate to make their products taste better or have a longer shelf life, or to make them cheaper to produce, can be cumulatively harmful to us.

Most of us know that if we throw too much fat left over from cooking animal products into our sink drains, the fat will congeal and eventually stick to the linings of the pipes, creating a blockage that will prevent the water from flowing through. The same type of thing happens to the blood vessels in our bodies if we eat too much solid fat, better known as saturated fat. Saturated fat, cholesterol, and triglyceride molecules, carried along in our blood, move through our blood vessels like water moves through pipes. And often, over time, if there is too much saturated fat circulating in our blood, as it migrates through our vessel walls, it tends to stick in our arteries in deposits known as plaque. These deposits create a narrowing and hardening of the "pipes" through which our blood must flow. The buildup of these soft, waxy plaque particles forms a blockage that can eventually cause a closure of one or more blood vessels, leading to a major medical problem, such as stroke or heart disease.

However, foods containing saturated fat may not be the only "culprits." Recent scientific studies reveal that the consumption of too many of what are called high glycemic carbohydrates—those found in refined flours, sugar, and grains (which are added in high amounts to processed, fast, and snack foods)—becomes potentially harmful to our bodies when they are transformed through the process of digestion. One of the major dangers they pose is that their high sugar content spikes insulin blood levels, and too much insulin production often leads to early-onset diabetes. Researchers have also found that consuming too many carbohydrate products in an attempt to avoid high-fat foods has led to an alarming increase of obesity throughout the American population.

While it is true that calories from carbohydrates measure about half those of fats, we cannot consume them in unlimited numbers. Eating more of them can actually make us feel hungrier—and the hungrier we become, the more of them we crave. Carbohydrates turn into blood sugars, which give the body energy. But eating too many of them causes an increase in insulin levels, which affects fat metabolism in such a way that the body cannot burn its own fat for fuel. And more harmful body fat is gained when excess or "hidden" carbohydrates in the form of processed, prepared, snack, and fast food are consumed. As if this vicious cycle were not enough, many so called fat-free carbohydrate products contain partially hydrogenated ingredients that raise unwanted triglyceride levels in our blood because the process of hydrogenation of even healthy ingredients turns them into unhealthy saturated fats.

COMPLICATED FACTS MADE SIMPLE

One of the most important things to remember is that NOT ALL FATS AND CARBOHYDRATES ARE HARMFUL. In fact, in order to maintain healthy bodies and metabolisms through balanced eating habits, it is ESSENTIAL that we consume some dietary fat and high-fiber carbohydrate on a daily basis. BUT, in regard to the question of fat, it is the type we eat that is important. As a rule, not more than 30% of the total number of calories we eat each day SHOULD contain fat. BUT of those, ONLY 10% or FEWER should be saturated fat. In other words, no more than 3% of our total daily calories should consist of saturated fat.

The kind and amount of fat in our blood is measured by our cholesterol and triglyceride levels. And, surprisingly, 80% of the cholesterol in our bodies is that which is produced naturally in our livers. The remaining 20% is what each of us is able to influence by our food choices. Why then is our consumption of dietary fat so important to our cholesterol levels? Because foods high in saturated fat can, without our even realizing it, raise our total blood levels above the danger zone of the medically recommended level of 200 milligrams.

Total cholesterol levels are broken down into several important numbers: LDL (or low density lipoproteins), known as "bad" cholesterol; HDL (or high density lipoproteins), known as "good" cholesterol; and triglycerides. Though our triglyceride numbers should be as low as possible, the higher our HDL number is compared to our LDL number, the better off we are. The most significant way in which we can keep these numbers in line so that our LDL measures 100 milligrams or less and our HDL measures 60 milligrams or higher is by consuming less saturated fat and fewer refined carbohydrates—and by making regular aerobic exercise part of our lives.

WHAT ARE THESE THINGS CALLED FATS AND CARBOHYDRATES?

While this cookbook is not a book about calories, it would be remiss not to reveal that the calories from fat (9 calories per gram) are MORE THAN DOUBLE those from either proteins or carbohydrates (4 calories per gram each). This means that the more fat we eat, the faster we will become fatter. And it is likely that a high level of fat in one's diet increases the risk of colon, breast, ovarian, and uterine cancer, as well as the incidence of stroke and heart disease. The following discussion of both fats and carbohydrates explains just what they are and how they work.

Basically, fat falls into three categories:

BEST

Monounsaturated: fats such as olive oil that are liquid at room temperature but become partly solid when refrigerated

GOOD

Polyunsaturated: fats such as corn oil or sesame oil that are liquid both at room temperature or when cold

BAD

Saturated: fats that may soften at room temperature but still remain solid. Some of the foods highest in saturated fat include beef, pork (with the exception of well-trimmed tenderloin), lamb, duck, the dark meat and skin of chicken and turkey, whole milk, butter, eggs, cream, cheese, coconut oil, palm oil, and lard. The consumption of these saturated fats, especially animal fats, raises blood triglyceride and LDL cholesterol levels more than anything else we can eat!

All fats contain approximately 120 calories per tablespoon. Some, such as the omega-3 trans fats found in salmon, mackerel, other oily types of fish, nuts (especially walnuts), and avocados, have been proven to be particularly beneficial because they actually discourage plaque formation, especially if eaten several times per week. In addition, because omega-3 trans fats have been found to be essential in promoting intelligence in infants, the U.S. government has recently mandated that this element, which is a natural component of human breast milk, be included in all infant formula.

The process of hydrogenation turns unsaturated fat into an especially unhealthy form of saturated fat. That is why it is ESSENTIAL that we read product package labels carefully in order to minimize consumption of products containing hydrogenated or partially hydrogenated ingredients—even if that same label boasts that the product contains no saturated fat or cholesterol! And be warned! One of the hazards of low-fat or nonfat prepared foods is that many contain high levels of salt and refined carbohydrates in the form of sucrose and fructose sweeteners and starch, which manufacturers add as an easy and inexpensive way to make up for whatever part of a product's tastiness is lost when its fat content is removed. In order to be sure of just what we are eating, it is important that we make an effort to try to cook as many meals at home as possible and to stock up on a good variety of interesting spices for seasoning whatever low-fat recipes we choose to make.

UNDERSTANDING CARBOHYDRATES

Unless one has specific dietary restrictions, some carbohydrates are needed as part of one's daily food intake—roughly 250 mg for those consuming 1,500 calories a day and 300 mg for those whose daily caloric intake is 2,000 calories. Though all carbohydrates turn into sugar during the process of digestion, carbohydrates found in refined or processed sugar, starches (especially white flour), grains such as white rice, sodas, juices, white potatoes, and candy, to name a few, fall under the category of high glycemic carbohydrates. Because they are quickly digested, a large intake of them can spike the level of blood sugar, calling forth a surge of insulin. Insulin is a natural substance in the body, but constant overproduction of it can lead to the onset of diabetes. It can also lead to obesity by provoking what is known as insulin resistance, a condition in which high levels of insulin make it easier for the body to store fat and harder to lose it. Conversely, low glycemic carbohydrates, such as nuts, whole grains, bran cereals, fresh fruit, and vegetables, contain more fiber, which makes them slower to digest, so that blood insulin levels are maintained on an even keel when sensible amounts of them are consumed.

In order to become familiar with the nutritional content of many common food items, the chart on page 11 contains an abbreviated list of the fat, calorie, and carbohydrate content of selected foods, all of which are expressed in the number of grams contained in one-ounce (or two-teaspoon) measurements.

It is important to keep in mind that all of the foods listed in the chart are in measurements of only one ounce, much less than our daily consumption of them. The numbers might not seem like much when they are expressed in such a small numerical unit, but if the total of what we eat on any given day exceeds the recommended fat, saturated fat, and carbohydrate numbers previously mentioned, attention must be paid to lowering our intake for the sake of better health and longevity.

Food Comparisons

MEAT, FISH AND POULTRY

(Please note that for this category there is no listing for carbohydrates because the food items under this particular listing do not contain any. All approximate units of measurement for total fat, saturated fat, and cholesterol are expressed in grams.)

1 OUNCE	CALORIES	TOTAL FAT	SATURATED FAT	CHOLESTEROL
skinless turkey breast	31	.2	0.1	18
skinless chicken breast	31	.4	0.1	16
pork tenderloin	80	6.2	2.2	20
fresh salmon	51	3	0.7	19
roast ham	70	5.3	1.9	16
porterhouse steak	77	6.25	2.5	19
regular ground chuck	88	7.5	3.1	24
rib lamb chop	106	9.8	4.3	22

DAIRY

	CALORIES	TOTAL FAT	SATURATED FAT	CHOLESTEROL	CARBOHYDRATES
light coffee cream	60	6	4	20	1.0
(regular all-purpose cream)	90	9	6	40	1.0
regular sour cream	61	5.9	3.7	13	1.2
(nonfat sour cream)	35	0	0	0	6.0
processed Swiss cheese	95	7.1	4.6	24	.6
American cheese	106	8.9	5.6	27	.5
regular cream cheese	99	9.9	4.3	31	.8
1 egg	75	5	1.6	213	.6

FAST FOOD VERSUS OUR FOOD

Fast food may be just that, BUT it's mostly just plain fat and refined carbohydrate, and it's usually loaded with salt. For example, a McDonald's Quarter Pounder with Cheese contains 530 calories (of which 270 are from fat), 30 grams of total fat, 13 grams of saturated fat, 38 grams of carbohydrate, and a whopping 1,290 milligrams of sodium (a number that is over one-half of the daily recommended allowance). A small 2.4-ounce serving of fries adds another 210 calories (90 of which are from fat), 10 grams total fat, 1.5 grams saturated fat, 26 carbohydrate grams, and 135 mg of salt. A twelve-ounce "child-size" glass of Coke contains no fat but is high in empty fructose-based sugar calories—110 to be exact—which adds on another 29 grams of carbohydrate. And a 6.3-ounce hot fudge sundae for dessert adds 340 calories (100 of which are from fat), 12 grams total fat, 9 grams saturated fat, 52 carbohydrate grams, and, believe it or not, 170 mg of salt! That means that in one meal alone, which many teenagers consider "just a snack," we can consume 1,190 calories full of far more fat (460 grams), carbohydrates (145 grams), and salt than nutrition!

HEALTHY HOMEMADE MEAL COMPARISON

- ¼ pound ground breast of turkey burger: 124 calories, .8 gram total fat, .4 gram saturated fat, 0 carbohydrates

- 1 whole wheat hamburger roll: approximately 115 calories, 2.2 grams total fat, trace amount saturated fat, and 22 grams of carbohydrate

- 1 slice low-fat (2% milk) Kraft American cheese: 50 calories, 3 grams total fat, 2 grams saturated fat, and 2 grams of carbohydrate

- carrot and celery sticks—no fat and few calories with a high fiber carbohydrate count of 31 grams (per medium carrot and 1.5 grams per stalk of celery)

- ½ cup unsweetened applesauce: 53 calories, no fat, and 13.8 grams of high fiber carbohydrates

- 8 ounces skim milk: 86 calories, .4 gram fat, .3 gram saturated fat, and 11.9 grams of carbohydrate

- ½ cup sherbet: 132 calories, 1.9 grams of fat, 1.2 grams of saturated fat, and 29 grams of carbohydrate

The results are astounding when you consider that a homemade meal such as the one above contains a total count of approximately 560 calories. The total fat count for the entire meal is less than 9 grams, of which less than 4 are saturated, and the total carbohydrate count, though only 33 grams less, is composed largely of food items high in fiber. In real terms, that means that not only does the McDonald's meal contain more than twice as many calories as the suggested homemade meal, it also contains over six times more total fat, and six times more saturated fat, and an excess of high glycemic carbohydrates!

Though the menu might sound a bit plain, the truth is that these choices may be made and presented in a tasty manner that is so much better for us and our families—and ultimately far more cost-efficient as well! And if at first our families need some extra coaxing to adjust to new and better healthy eating habits, try to think of creative ways to arrange and present food that will give it added eye appeal. While it is true that this sample menu doesn't offer much of a culinary challenge beyond adding seasonings of choice to the turkey burger, not everything has to be so plain and simple. In fact, the easy-to-follow suggestions and substitutions listed in the recipes throughout this book will demonstrate how to make healthy changes to many of the dishes that might be similar to those that are already our standard favorites.

The way food is prepared in each of our own kitchens greatly influences its effect on the body. Frying, even with nonsaturated oil, means that the foods prepared in this way have a higher degree of fat content and more calories in them than, for example, foods that are baked or broiled. The same holds true for foods that call for sautéing, browning, or softening in fats or oils, steps that can easily be replaced or eliminated altogether. Throughout the mouthwatering new and appealing recipes within these pages, you will also learn techniques that will enable you to make adjustments to many of your personal recipe favorites, so they become healthier for you and your family to consume.

A·B·C: THE EASY THREE—PLUS D

ALWAYS sweat the small stuff! This means that instead of the butter or other fats a recipe might call for to soften, brown, or sauté ingredients, there is a better, healthier alternative that gets the job done. Simply cover the bottom of a nonstick pan with 1 teaspoon of unsaturated oil or a light coating of cooking spray, heat slightly, and add your ingredients. Cook until the desired degree of softness is obtained by stirring the ingredients over low heat and adding 1 to 2 tablespoons of hot water to the pan EACH TIME it seems that the ingredients are beginning to dry out.

B

BUY at least one very good nonstick pot or pan—and the proper utensils to use with it, so that the surface doesn't get broken or become scratched. It is always best to care for these pots by washing them by hand instead of putting them in a dishwasher. When cleaning them, never use anything abrasive that will scratch the delicately coated cooking surface of your utensil. Most important of all, NEVER, NEVER, put a hot pot with a nonstick surface directly into the sink after use. Contact with cool tap water will result in a cracking of the surface. One last hint that will add to the longevity of your cookware is to place a piece of paper toweling over the nonstick surface to provide protection from any potential damage from other cookware in your storage cabinet.

C

CONSTANTLY read labels when buying food to be sure that the product on which you are spending your money is really good for you and your family. Many labels are tricky—sometimes intentionally so—and it takes a lot of learning, practice, and patience to become knowledgeable in the art of making good food choices.

D

DON'T FORGET—it's all about numbers. Try to familiarize yourself with the nutritional components of the foods you serve your family each day to be sure they "add up" properly for the sake of their health—and yours! Most grocery products—with the exception of fresh meat, fruit, and vegetables—have detailed nutritional information listed on their packaging. Each product is required by law to list every ingredient in descending order, which means that the most abundant ingredient is mentioned at the beginning and the least abundant ingredient is listed at the end.

GETTING STARTED

Now that we know our A,B,C, and Ds, it's time to get started by using substitution rather than abstinence as your key. Listed below are but a few recommended healthy alternatives to use in place of many similar common daily food items. (Of course, fresh fruits and vegetables are always daily essentials.)

- nonfat mayonnaise spread
- non-dairy cream that is not hydrogenated
- nonhydrogenated butter substitute
- liquid egg substitutes
- low-fat or nonfat milk
- nonfat half-and-half that is also nonhydrogenated
- olive or other nonsaturated oil
- nonfat stocks such as chicken, beef, or vegetable
- low-fat cream cheese
- low-fat or nonfat sour cream
- turkey bacon or turkey deli meats
- unrefined or whole wheat carbohydrate products
- as many interesting spices as you can imagine—
  variety is the spice of life—and cooking too!

Many of these substitutions—and others as well—will already be incorporated into the recipes throughout this book. Notes in italics will not only indicate these changes but will often provide interesting meal planning and menu suggestions to accompany the dish being prepared. These recipes are delicious, easy to prepare, and most of all, beneficial for you and your family. And with just a little practice, it won't be long before you will be able to look at a recipe that's a "baddie" and be able to change it to one that's a more healthful "goodie."

Patti Sowalsky

Patti Sowalsky

About the Author

Patti Sowalsky, a resident of Potomac, Maryland,
has had a lifelong interest in cooking and the development
of healthy recipes. She previously coauthored and published
On Exhibit, an annual guide to American art museums,
and undertook the two-year effort to write this book to make
readers aware that healthy cooking need not be dull and bland
but can be interesting, tasty, and fun.

Patti dedicates this book to the future health of the
youth of the Boys & Girls Clubs of Greater Washington
and those who guide them.

Starters

starters

Tuscan White Bean Salad

Serves 4

INGREDIENTS

1 (16-ounce) can	cannellini beans—rinsed and drained
1 large rib	celery—cut on the diagonal into the thinnest slices possible
1/4 small	red onion—cut into the thinnest slices possible
1 to 2 Tablespoons	fresh Italian parsley—finely chopped
1 Tablespoon	lemon juice
2 Tablespoons	olive oil
1/4 teaspoon	(or less) kosher salt
freshly ground white pepper to taste	
10	cherry tomatoes—cut in halves

METHOD

1. Place all of the ingredients, except for the tomatoes, in a bowl, and mix them together thoroughly.
2. Cover the bowl and place the mix in the refrigerator for several hours to chill.
3. When ready to use, mix in the tomatoes and serve.

NOTES

An ideal starter, this refreshing good-for-you bean preparation, high in protein and dietary fiber, is also the perfect accompaniment to a meal of simply grilled fish or chicken. Because beans are also high in carbohydrates, care must be taken to avoid serving this salad with other high carbohydrate foods, such as bread.

NUTRIENTS PER SERVING

CAL	PROT	CARBO	T FAT	SAT. FAT	CAL FROM FAT	CHOL	FIBER	SOD
162	5G	19G	7G	1G	41%	0MG	5G	372MG

Cocktail Olives

Serves 6

INGREDIENTS

1 teaspoon	olive oil
1 Tablespoon	freshly chopped garlic
1 Tablespoon	herbes de Provence
skin of 1 lemon—removed with a zester tool	
1/2 pound	oil-cured olives

NOTES

Always popular as a cocktail or snack item, the flavor of this olive mix improves when stored in the refrigerator for at least 24 hours before serving. When ready to use, the olives should be removed from the refrigerator in time for them to be brought to room temperature.

NUTRIENTS PER SERVING

CAL	PROT	CARBO	T FAT	SAT. FAT	CAL FROM FAT	CHOL	FIBER	SOD
228	‹1G	9G	17G	1G	80%	0MG	3G	891MG

METHOD

1. Heat the olive oil in a small nonstick pan.
2. Add the garlic, herbes de Provence and lemon and "sweat" them on low heat. Stir them occasionally until they soften and are lightly browned.
3. Add the olives and stir them into the garlic mix over low heat until just heated through.
4. Remove the pan from the heat and, when cool, transfer the olives to a covered dish and refrigerate until ready to use.

Roasted Cocktail Peanuts

INGREDIENTS

1 cup	salted (or unsalted if preferred) peanuts

NOTES

It is hard to believe that the rich taste of these nuts is created by simple roasting without any additional fats or oils. However, this recipe is NOT successful if dry roasted nuts are used. During the roasting process, close observation is important to ensure that the nuts, which are prone to burning, are removed from the heat before they become too dark and bitter tasting. If purchased in large amounts, extra uncooked nuts may be stored in the freezer for freshness. The unsaturated fat in peanuts and many other nuts makes them an ideal healthy snack to have on hand. However, it is important to eat them in moderation because, though high in protein and other nutrients, they are also high in calories–165 to be exact–per one ounce, or 28 peanuts.

METHOD

1. Spread the nuts evenly across a metal tray.
2. Place them in a 325-degree oven and, shaking them occasionally, roast them for 10 to 15 minutes or until the nuts turn deep golden in color.
3. Remove them from the oven and let cool before serving.

NUTRIENTS PER SERVING

CAL	PROT	CARBO	T FAT	SAT. FAT	CAL FROM FAT	CHOL	FIBER	SOD
139	6G	5G	12G	2G	71%	0MG	2G	104MG

Artichoke Dip

Serves 6

INGREDIENTS

4 slices	turkey bacon
½ cup	low-fat mayonnaise
1 Tablespoon	lemon juice
1 (8-ounce) can	hearts of artichoke—drain, pat dry and cut each heart into small pieces
1 Tablespoon	minced dehydrated onion

NOTES

Serving with baked tortilla chips gives this dip added zing. Turkey bacon is best when cooked in a microwave oven. It can also be prepared by placing the strips in a nonstick pan and cooking them on low heat on a stovetop burner. If desired, before serving prepare 2 more strips of turkey bacon to crumble and use as a garnish on top of the dip.

METHOD

1. Cook the turkey bacon—in a microwave if possible—until it is crisp. When done, blot the slices dry and set them aside.
2. Place the low-fat mayonnaise in a deep bowl and beat the lemon juice into it.
3. Add the artichokes and the dehydrated onion to #2 and mix well.
4. Crumble the turkey bacon, mix it into #3, cover the bowl with plastic wrap and refrigerate overnight.
5. Before serving, stir the ingredients together once again.

NUTRIENTS PER SERVING

CAL	PROT	CARBO	T FAT	SAT. FAT	CAL FROM FAT	CHOL	FIBER	SOD
110	3G	6G	8G	2G	67%	14MG	1G	502MG

Avocado Dip

Serves 8

INGREDIENTS

2 large	ripe avocados–peeled and cut into 1/8ths
1/2 large	Vidalia (or other sweet) onion–peeled and cut into chunks
juice of 1 lime	
kosher salt and freshly ground black pepper to taste	

METHOD

1. Place all of the ingredients in a food processor and pulse them until the desired consistency (either chunky or smooth) is reached.
2. The dip may either be chilled in the refrigerator until ready to use, or it may be served at room temperature.

NOTES

Because avocados are high in good-for-you omega-3 trans fatty acid, this easy recipe makes for an ideal snack or hors d'oeuvre—especially when served on whole wheat pita bread. For a change of pace, try adding 1/2 teaspoon (plus or minus) of dried cumin to the recipe.

NUTRIENTS PER SERVING

CAL	PROT	CARBO	T FAT	SAT. FAT	CAL FROM FAT	CHOL	FIBER	SOD
91	2G	6G	8G	2G	70%	0MG	5G	‹1MG

Very Low-Fat Crab Dip

Serves at least 12

INGREDIENTS

1 Tablespoon	nonhydrogenated butter substitute
¼ cup	scallions—finely chopped
3 Tablespoons	celery—minced
1 Tablespoon	green bell pepper—diced
1 Tablespoon	red bell pepper—diced
2 cloves	garlic—minced
1½ Tablespoons	flour
8 large	mushrooms—washed, blotted dry on paper toweling and thinly sliced
⅔ cup	evaporated skim milk
1 teaspoon	white wine
2 Tablespoons	dry sherry
1 teaspoon	Worcestershire sauce
½ teaspoon	Tabasco sauce
1 teaspoon	onion powder
1 teaspoon	crushed dried basil
kosher salt and freshly ground black pepper to taste	
8 ounces	fat-free cream cheese
1 pound	lump crabmeat—drained and flaked

METHOD

1. Melt the butter substitute in a nonstick skillet.
2. Stir in the scallions, peppers, celery and garlic and cook 5 minutes on low to medium heat.
3. Add the flour and cook 3 minutes, stirring constantly.
4. Add the mushrooms and cook 1 minute more.
5. Remove the skillet from the heat. Then stir the milk, wine, dry sherry, Worcestershire and Tabasco sauce into the pan.
6. Return the skillet to the heat and cook 1½ to 2 minutes.
7. Season the mix by stirring in the onion powder, basil, salt and pepper.
8. Add the cream cheese in pieces and stir until it is melted.
9. Stir in the crabmeat, cook 2 minutes more, and serve hot.

NOTES

Served with crackers or whole wheat pita slices, this warm, easy to make, one-pan hors d'oeuvre is the hit of any party.

NUTRIENTS PER SERVING

CAL	PROT	CARBO	T FAT	SAT. FAT	CAL FROM FAT	CHOL	FIBER	SOD
80	11G	5G	1G	‹1G	15%	31MG	‹1G	235MG

Shrimp Dip

Serves 8

INGREDIENTS

¼ pound	low-fat cream cheese
2 Tablespoons	low-fat mayonnaise
1 Tablespoon	Worcestershire sauce
1 Tablespoon	onion—finely grated
1 medium-sized	ripe tomato—peeled, seeded and chopped
¾ cup	shrimp—cooked, cleaned and chopped

METHOD

1. Bring the cream cheese to room temperature.
2. In a bowl combine the cream cheese, mayonnaise, Worcestershire sauce and onion.
3. Mix in the tomato and shrimp, cover the bowl, and refrigerate until ready to serve.

NOTES

Celery sticks are perfect scoops for this easy-to-make hors d'oeuvre. Or for a more elegant presentation, spread the dip on spears of endive and arrange them artfully on a flat platter.

NUTRIENTS PER SERVING

CAL	PROT	CARBO	T FAT	SAT. FAT	CAL FROM FAT	CHOL	FIBER	SOD
65	5G	2G	4G	2G	55%	39MG	‹1G	128MG

Fresh and Lively Salsa

Serves 4

INGREDIENTS

10	ripe Roma tomatoes–coarsely chopped
1 medium to large	red onion–coarsely chopped
1 bunch	fresh cilantro–washed, dried and minced
2 cloves	fresh garlic–crushed in a garlic press
2 Tablespoons	fresh lime juice
1 Tablespoon	white vinegar
2 teaspoons	sea or coarse salt
1 teaspoon	red pepper flakes
$1/8$ teaspoon (or more to taste) hot sauce	
1 teaspoon	ground cumin

METHOD

1. Mix all of the ingredients together in a deep bowl, cover and refrigerate at least 1 hour before serving.

NOTES

Whatever liquid that collects as the salsa is chilling should be drained off before serving. After draining, the salsa might have to be corrected for seasoning according to taste. One of the most nutritious and popular of all hors d'oeuvre items, salsa may also be used as a side dish for grilled fish or as a filler for baked potatoes.

NUTRIENTS PER SERVING

CAL	PROT	CARBO	T FAT	SAT. FAT	CAL FROM FAT	CHOL	FIBER	SOD
65	2G	15G	1G	‹1G	8%	‹1MG	3G	1175MG

Greek-Style Cauliflower Spread

Serves 8

INGREDIENTS

2 large	heads fresh cauliflower
6 cloves	(plus or minus) garlic–peeled
3 cups	nonfat chicken broth
3 ounces	feta cheese
1 teaspoon	dried oregano
1/8 teaspoon	kosher salt
1/8 teaspoon	(plus or minus) freshly ground black pepper

METHOD

1. Cut the cauliflower, discard the stems and place the florets in a deep pot.
2. Add the garlic cloves and chicken broth, bring the liquid to a boil, cover and simmer 50 minutes until the cauliflower is soft.
3. Remove the pot from the heat and let the contents cool.
4. Drain off and discard the liquid.
5. Place the cauliflower, garlic, feta cheese, oregano and salt and pepper in a food processor and blend until smooth.
6. Transfer the mix to a bowl, cover and refrigerate until ready to serve.

NOTES

Only the top part of each head of cauliflower is used in this preparation. This dish, which is best served on small pieces of whole wheat pita bread or on thin slices of sourdough bread, may be kept in the refrigerator for up to a week. Garlic lovers may add an additional 1/2 or whole fresh clove of garlic if desired when the mix is being processed.

NUTRIENTS PER SERVING

CAL	PROT	CARBO	T FAT	SAT. FAT	CAL FROM FAT	CHOL	FIBER	SOD
90	7G	12G	3G	2G	24%	9MG	5G	444MG

Lite and Luscious Cocktail Cheese Spread

Serves 10

INGREDIENTS

3 ounces	low-fat cream cheese
6 Tablespoons	nonhydrogenated butter substitute
½ teaspoon	anchovy paste (or more to taste)
1 Tablespoon	onion–grated
1 teaspoon	paprika
1 teaspoon	(plus or minus) caraway seeds

METHOD

1. Place the cream cheese in a bowl and bring it to room temperature.
2. Add the rest of the ingredients and mix them all together with a fork until they are well combined.
3. Refrigerate until ready to use.

NOTES

This zesty and delicious spread lasts for 2 weeks in the refrigerator. It is tastiest when served just out of the refrigerator. It takes a bit of "elbow grease" to mash the ingredients together so they are well integrated to the point where only small flecks of the white cream cheese are visible. Traditional versions of this spread call for regular cream cheese and butter—but this one is equal to the original in taste—and better for you!

NUTRIENTS PER SERVING

CAL	PROT	CARBO	T FAT	SAT. FAT	CAL FROM FAT	CHOL	FIBER	SOD
69	1G	1G	7G	2G	89%	5MG	‹1G	79MG

Eggplant Caponata

Serves 8

INGREDIENTS

2 Tablespoons	olive oil
1 medium	eggplant—peeled and cubed
1 medium	onion—chopped
1/3 cup	green bell pepper—seeded and chopped
1 celery	rib—chopped
2 cloves	garlic—minced
1/2 cup	green olives with pimentos—chopped
1/4 pound	fresh or canned mushrooms—chopped
1 (6-ounce) can	tomato paste
3/4 cup	water
1 1/2 teaspoons	sugar
2 Tablespoons	red vinegar
1/2 teaspoon	(plus or minus) dried oregano
1 Tablespoon	small capers
1/2 teaspoon	(plus or minus) dried cumin
2 to 3 Tablespoons pine nuts—lightly toasted	

METHOD

1. Spread the olive oil over the bottom of a deep nonstick pot. Add the eggplant, onion, green pepper, celery, garlic, olives and mushrooms, heat and cook the mix on low for 10 minutes. Add 2 to 3 Tablespoons of water if the ingredients become dry.

2. Stir in the tomato paste, water, sugar, red vinegar, oregano, capers and cumin, cover, bring the ingredients to a simmer and cook 20 minutes.

3. Remove the pot from the heat and, when cool, stir in the pine nuts.

4. Transfer the caponata to a covered bowl and refrigerate 24 hours before using to allow the flavors to become fully integrated.

NOTES

A terrific party appetizer or picnic item, this recipe is a natural for spreading on slices of crusty sourdough bread. The advantage to preparing this recipe several days in advance of use is that the longer the caponata is refrigerated, the better the flavors blend. This recipe also lends itself quite well to canning. For variety when serving, try placing a generous spoonful of hot caponata inside of a baked potato or use it as a sauce for whole wheat pasta. It also perfectly complements grilled fish when served as a side dish.

NUTRIENTS PER SERVING

CAL	PROT	CARBO	T FAT	SAT. FAT	CAL FROM FAT	CHOL	FIBER	SOD
109	3G	12G	7G	1G	49%	0MG	3G	357MG

Salmon Log with Walnuts

Serves 8

INGREDIENTS

1 pound can	salmon
1/2 pound package	low-fat cream cheese
1 Tablespoon	fresh lemon juice
2 teaspoons	onion—finely grated
1 teaspoon	white horseradish (or more to taste)
1/2 cup	walnuts—chopped
3 Tablespoons	fresh parsley—chopped

NOTES

This flavorful preparation never fails to please as an hors d'oeuvre that can be used from brunch through evening cocktails. Both the salmon and the walnuts contain beneficial omega-3 trans fatty acids, making this an especially good-for-you treat.

METHOD

1. Drain the salmon, remove the skin and bones, and place the salmon in a bowl.
2. Add the cream cheese, lemon juice, onion and horseradish to the salmon and combine thoroughly.
3. Shape #2 into a log, cover and refrigerate—overnight if possible.
4. Combine the walnuts and parsley and spread this mix on a piece of waxed paper.
5. Roll the chilled salmon log over the mix to coat entire surface of the log.
6. Cover and refrigerate the completed log until ready to serve.

NUTRIENTS PER SERVING

CAL	PROT	CARBO	T FAT	SAT. FAT	CAL FROM FAT	CHOL	FIBER	SOD
179	18G	3G	11G	4G	54%	56MG	‹1G	307MG

Hummus

Serves 10

INGREDIENTS

1 large clove	fresh garlic—finely minced
1 (20-ounce) can	garbanzo beans—rinsed and drained
1 teaspoon	kosher salt
freshly ground black pepper to taste	
1/3 cup	olive oil
1 teaspoon	ground cumin (or more to taste)
juice of 1 lemon	

METHOD

1. Place the garlic in a food processor and pulse until it is minced.
2. Add the rest of the ingredients and process until the mix is puréed and is creamy in texture.
3. Correct for seasoning according to your taste and refrigerate the hummus until ready to serve.

NOTES

During the process of puréeing, if the mix does not appear to be creamy enough, additional olive oil may be required. If so, it should be added—a little at a time—during the blending process until the desired consistency of creaminess is achieved. In addition to serving hummus on small whole wheat pita bread rounds, it may be used a dip for carrots, celery, broccoli and other hard vegetables of choice.

NUTRIENTS PER SERVING

CAL	PROT	CARBO	T FAT	SAT. FAT	CAL FROM FAT	CHOL	FIBER	SOD
133	3G	13G	8G	1G	52%	0MG	3G	358MG

Old-Fashioned Ham Salad

Serves 4

INGREDIENTS

1 (6-ounce) package smoked, low-sugar ham slices	
2 Tablespoons	nonfat mayonnaise (or more to taste)
2 Tablespoons	sugar-free dill relish (or more to taste)

METHOD

1. Coarsely chop the ham slices, place them in a food processor and pulse them until the meat is finely ground.
2. Transfer the ham to a bowl, mix in the rest of the ingredients, cover and chill in the refrigerator at least 1 hour before serving.

NOTES

Rich in taste but not in content, this versatile preparation may be spread on spears of endive for an elegant presentation, piled into hard-boiled egg whites for more casual dining or simply scooped up with celery sticks for a snack on the run. It also makes for a tasty sandwich when served on hearty rye or pumpernickel bread with lettuce and ripe tomato slices.

NUTRIENTS PER SERVING

CAL	PROT	CARBO	T FAT	SAT. FAT	CAL FROM FAT	CHOL	FIBER	SOD
46	7G	1G	2G	‹1G	30%	20MG	0G	644MG

Tomato Tapenade

Serves 6

INGREDIENTS

3 ounces	sun-dried tomatoes
1 Tablespoon	small capers
2 teaspoon	garlic, chopped
1 teaspoon	fresh lemon rind—grated
1 teaspoon	fresh lemon juice
1/2 teaspoon	herbes de Provence
1 teaspoon	olive oil

METHOD

1. Soften the tomatoes by soaking them for at least 10 minutes in very hot water.
2. Drain off the water and blot the tomatoes on paper toweling.
3. Place the tomatoes in a bowl, drizzle the olive oil over them and let them sit for approximately 1 hour to let the oil penetrate into the tomato flesh.
4. Place the tomatoes and the rest of the ingredients in a food processor and pulse until mix is well combined.
5. Store the tapenade in a covered container in the refrigerator until ready to use.

NOTES

If desired, a bit of salt may be added to taste. A tangy treat, this preparation may be stored in the refrigerator for up to two weeks. It makes a tasty hors d'oeuvre when spread in a thin layer on small, plain crackers or toasts.

NUTRIENTS PER SERVING

CAL	PROT	CARBO	T FAT	SAT. FAT	CAL FROM FAT	CHOL	FIBER	SOD
47	2G	9G	1G	‹1G	20%	0MG	2G	340MG

Onion Marmalade

Serves 15

INGREDIENTS

4 pounds	onions—cut into quarters and thinly sliced
1 Tablespoon	olive oil
1 teaspoon	salt
freshly ground pepper to taste	
1 cup	red wine vinegar
2¼ cups	nonfat chicken broth
1 Tablespoon	sugar

METHOD

1. Mix all of the ingredients together in a large, ovenproof glass bowl.
2. Place the bowl UNCOVERED in a microwave oven and cook—stirring occasionally—on high power for at least 60 minutes or until none of the liquid remains and the onions begin to brown and caramelize.
3. When done, remove the onions from the microwave, let them cool and refrigerate them until ready to use.

NOTES

While cooking, the onions should be checked and mixed after approximately 40 minutes and then again every ten minutes until done. Be careful when mixing to avoid the live steam that rises from the bowl. This preparation may be refrigerated for up to two weeks. It is a perfect "anytime" snack when served on plain small whole wheat crackers.

NUTRIENTS PER SERVING

CAL	PROT	CARBO	T FAT	SAT. FAT	CAL FROM FAT	CHOL	FIBER	SOD
65	2G	13G	1G	‹1G	14%	0MG	2G	253MG

Asparagus and Potato Frittata

Serves 6

INGREDIENTS

³/₄ pound	fresh asparagus
2 Tablespoons	olive oil
3	scallions–remove the top 3rd of each scallion and finely chop the remaining ²/₃
8 small	unpeeled new potatoes–washed, dried and cut across the width into thin coin-like slices
1 teaspoon	(plus or minus) dried or freshly chopped tarragon
kosher salt and freshly ground black pepper to taste	
2³/₄ cups	egg substitute
¹/₃ cup	freshly grated Parmesan cheese (or more to taste)
3 Tablespoons	nonhydrogenated butter substitute
¹/₂ cup	low-fat Swiss cheese–shredded

METHOD

1. Wash the asparagus and snap off and discard the tough ends.
2. Drop the asparagus spears in boiling water and cook for no more than 2 minutes.
3. Immediately drain them into a colander then transfer them to a bowl of ice water to stop the cooking process.
4. When cool, remove the asparagus from the water, dry them, cut them into thin 2- to 3-inch slices and set them aside.
5. Heat 1 Tablespoon of olive oil in a 10- to 12-inch nonstick fry pan, add the scallions and "sweat" them, stirring occasionally, until they soften.
6. Add the potatoes, tarragon, salt, pepper and 1 more Tablespoon of olive oil to the pan and cook several minutes more until the potatoes look slightly glazed.
7. Cover the pan and continue cooking 10 minutes more, shaking the pan occasionally, until the potatoes become tender. If needed, add a bit more oil during this process to prevent the potatoes from sticking.
8. Uncover the pan and continue cooking until the potatoes appear to brown.
9. Remove the pan from the heat, transfer the potatoes to the bowl with the asparagus and set the mix aside.

10. Pour the egg substitute into a large bowl and mix with a whisk.

11. Blend in the Parmesan cheese and the salt and pepper to taste.

12. Using the same nonstick frying pan, heat the nonhydrogenated butter substitute and, when melted, add the egg mix.

13. Cook the egg mix for 3 to 4 minutes on medium heat, taking care to lift around the edges with a rubber spatula as the eggs cook in order to allow the still-liquid parts on top to run underneath and come in contact with the hot surface of the pan.

14. Spread the potato and asparagus combination and the Swiss cheese evenly across the top of the still-softened egg and cook 3 to 4 minutes more.

15. Remove the pan from the burner and, if the handle is not heatproof, wrap it with aluminum foil.

16. Turn the oven on broil, place the pan on a rack in the oven that is close to the flame and, watching carefully, allow the eggs to cook until the top is evenly browned.

17. Slide the frittata onto a platter, cut into wedges and serve at once.

Photograph for this recipe appears on page 18.

NOTES

Steps 1 through 9 may be prepared in advance. If stored in the refrigerator prior to using, be sure to allow enough time to let the mix reach room temperature before cooking. Frittata creations are as varied as your imagination. Many other seasonal and herb combinations may be added to the egg base according to personal preference. In addition to brunch, frittatas make a wonderful main course supper item when served for nutritional balance with a crunchy green salad and a slice or two of sourdough bread. The measurements for this recipe may easily be cut in half and cooked in an 8-inch pan to accommodate fewer diners. It is important that this recipe be made with new potatoes. Unlike other white potatoes, they are made up of a different molecular structure that is absorbed more slowly by the body and therefore does not cause an insulin spike during the process of digestion.

NUTRIENTS PER SERVING

CAL	PROT	CARBO	T FAT	SAT. FAT	CAL FROM FAT	CHOL	FIBER	SOD
287	21G	31G	11G	3G	32%	7MG	4G	384MG

Crisp Baked Parmesan Cheese Rounds

Serves 5

INGREDIENTS

⅓ pound	freshly grated Parmigiano-Reggiano cheese

NOTES

No one will believe that these tasty little rounds are so simple to make. And because they are made out of such a hard cheese product, they contain the least amount of saturated fat of any of the cheeses. The rounds may be made in advance of use and simply stored at room temperature on a plate covered with aluminum foil. They may be eaten plain as a snack or cocktail item or served as an accompaniment to a tossed green or other salad of choice.

METHOD

1. Preheat the oven to 325 degrees.
2. Cover a large metal baking sheet with heavy-duty aluminum foil.
3. Coat the foil evenly with a thin layer of cooking spray.
4. Place a heaping Tablespoon of cheese on a portion of the foil and spread it into a uniformly thin, round layer. There should be enough room on a large pan for at least 10 spoonfuls.
5. Set the pan in the oven and let the cheese melt until it is slightly browned and bubbling.
6. Remove the pan from the oven and let the rounds cool before carefully removing them from the foil.

NUTRIENTS PER SERVING

CAL	PROT	CARBO	T FAT	SAT. FAT	CAL FROM FAT	CHOL	FIBER	SOD
138	13G	1G	9G	6G	60%	24MG	0G	563MG

Gravlax

Serves 10 (depending on whether it is used as an hors d'oeuvre or as a main course dinner item)

INGREDIENTS

1 (1½-pound) fillet of salmon–skin left on the bottom	
2 Tablespoons	kosher salt
1 teaspoon	sugar
½ teaspoon	ground cloves
lots of freshly ground black pepper	
¾ of large bunch of fresh dill–remove heavy stems, wash, dry well and finely chop	
3 Tablespoons	Cognac

METHOD

1. Place the washed and dried salmon fillet (skin side down) on a large piece of plastic wrap.
2. In the following order, evenly coat the top of the fillet with the salt, sugar, ground cloves and ground pepper.
3. Next spread the top of the fillet with dill.
4. Lastly, sprinkle the top of the fish with Cognac and close the plastic wrap securely around the fillet.
5. Place the wrapped salmon on a flat tray and cover the top with another flat tray so that the fish is sandwiched in between.
6. Transfer #5 to the refrigerator and weight the top tray with a heavy object.
7. The fish will be ready to serve within 24 hours. It will last in the refrigerator for approximately 2 weeks and may be frozen as well.

NOTES

When ready to serve, scrape the coating off of the top of that portion of the fish you will be using. Then with a sharp non-serrated knife, cut the fish on the diagonal into very thin slices. Gravlax is as good for dinner served with fresh vegetables as it is for brunch served with egg white or egg substitute omelets and thinly sliced toasted bagels. It also makes an excellent hors d'oeuvre when each slice is placed on a cocktail-sized square of pumpernickel bread topped with a dollop of nonfat yogurt mustard sauce with dill (see recipe page 40). Even though it is not cooked, the heart-healthy salmon used in this preparation is not raw. The salt placed on top of the fillet acts to "cure" the fish as it melts down through the flesh during the first 24 hours it is in the refrigerator.

NUTRIENTS PER SERVING

CAL	PROT	CARBO	T FAT	SAT. FAT	CAL FROM FAT	CHOL	FIBER	SOD
134	15G	‹1G	6G	1G	43%	49MG	‹1G	1167MG

Fat-Free Yogurt Dill Sauce

Serves 6

INGREDIENTS

6 Tablespoons	nonfat plain yogurt
juice of ¹⁄₂ lime	
1 Tablespoon	Dijon mustard
4 to 6 Tablespoons fresh dill—finely chopped	

METHOD

1. Place all of the ingredients in a bowl and blend them together.

NOTES

This tangy sauce is as good on plain grilled salmon as it is served with gravlax. It may be assembled and chilled up to two days in advance of use.

NUTRIENTS PER SERVING

CAL	PROT	CARBO	T FAT	SAT. FAT	CAL FROM FAT	CHOL	FIBER	SOD
10	1G	2G	‹1G	‹1G	17%	‹1MG	‹1G	72MG

Cocktail Turkey Meatballs

As a cocktail item this recipe easily serves 12

INGREDIENTS FOR MEATBALLS

2 pounds	ground turkey breast
1	egg white
1/2 cup	plain bread crumbs
1 small	onion—grated
kosher salt and freshly ground black pepper to taste	

INGREDIENTS FOR SAUCE

1 (12-ounce) bottle chili sauce (reduced-sugar variety if available)	
1 (15-ounce) jar	reduced-sugar grape jelly
juice of 1 lemon	

METHOD

1. Mix all of the turkey meatball ingredients together.
2. Place all of the sauce ingredients in a deep saucepot and cook until they are well incorporated and the mix is hot.
3. With your hands, form small turkey balls approximately 1 inch in diameter and drop each into the hot sauce mix.
4. When all the turkey meatballs have been added, continue cooking for 20 to 25 minutes more so that they are all cooked through.
5. Serve hot by placing the turkey balls and sauce in a heatproof bowl.

NOTES

Formerly made with beef, this dish actually improves in flavor when frozen for a short period of time before using.

NUTRIENTS PER SERVING

CAL	PROT	CARBO	T FAT	SAT. FAT	CAL FROM FAT	CHOL	FIBER	SOD
129	2G	30G	<1G	<1G	2%	2MG	1G	991MG

Middle Eastern Turkey Meatballs

Serves 6

INGREDIENTS

1 pound	ground turkey breast
1 medium	onion–finely chopped
1 clove	fresh garlic–finely chopped or pressed
2 to 3 teaspoons	cumin
1/2 teaspoon	cinnamon
1/2 teaspoon	allspice
2 teaspoons	dried mint
2 Tablespoons	fresh chopped mint
1/3 cup	plain bread crumbs
1	egg white
1 teaspoon	kosher salt
freshly ground black pepper to taste	

METHOD

1. Place all of the ingredients in a large bowl and mix them until they are well blended.

2. Cover the bowl and refrigerate the mix several hours until it is well chilled.

3. When ready to cook, coat a 10- to 12-inch nonstick pan with cooking spray (or 1 Tablespoon olive oil if preferred) and set the heat on low.

4. Using your hands, form small (approximately 1 1/2 inches in diameter) balls of the turkey mix and add them to the pan.

5. Cook them on low heat, turning them often so that all sides of each meatball are cooked through and slightly browned.

6. When done, remove them from the heat and serve.

NOTES

This recipe, traditionally made with ground lamb, is so rich with the flavor of cumin and mint that the substitution of lean turkey for high-fat lamb will hardly be noticed. If not serving the meatballs immediately, they may be refrigerated and later heated in the microwave—or they may be frozen. When freezing, it is important to lay the meatballs out on a platter so that they are separated and do not stick together in the freezing process. Once frozen, they can all be transferred to an airtight plastic ziplock bag. Plastic teaspoons make ideal implements for turning the meatballs as they cook. They are easy to use and will not damage the delicate coated surface of the nonstick pan.

NUTRIENTS PER SERVING

CAL	PROT	CARBO	T FAT	SAT. FAT	CAL FROM FAT	CHOL	FIBER	SOD
94	16G	6G	1G	‹1G	8%	35MG	‹1G	403MG

Oven-Dried Tomatoes

Serves 6

INGREDIENTS

1 Tablespoon	(or more as desired) olive oil
10	ripe Roma tomatoes
1 to 2 Tablespoons	garlic–freshly chopped
1 teaspoon	herbes de Provence
kosher salt and freshly ground black pepper to taste	

NOTES

Oven drying concentrates the flavor of the tomato by reducing its moisture content. These intensely flavorful tidbits store well in the refrigerator and may be used as accents in salads, or as cocktail items when placed on small toasted slices of sourdough bread spread with a thin layer of goat cheese and shreds of fresh basil. The tomatoes may be stored for up to two weeks in the refrigerator.

NUTRIENTS PER SERVING

CAL	PROT	CARBO	T FAT	SAT. FAT	CAL FROM FAT	CHOL	FIBER	SOD
51	1G	7G	3G	‹1G	42%	0MG	1G	10MG

METHOD

1. Preheat the oven to 325 degrees.
2. Line a metal cooking sheet with heavy-duty aluminum foil and spread the oil over the surface of the foil.
3. Wash and dry the tomatoes, cut a small thin slice off of the length of the side of each one, then cut each tomato in half lengthwise.
4. Lay the tomato halves on the foil and coat both sides with the oil.
5. With the large surface of each of the halves facing up, spread the surface with the garlic, herbes de Provence, salt and pepper.
6. Place the tomatoes in the oven to slow roast 1 hour or more until they appear to become somewhat dry and soft. During the cooking process, try to keep the tomatoes from sticking to the foil by occasionally moving them with a spatula.
7. When done, remove the slices from the oven and place them on a plate to cool.

Chilled Gazpacho

Serves 8

INGREDIENTS

3 medium-sized	ripe tomatoes–cut into quarters
1 medium	green bell pepper–seeded and cut into chunks
1 medium	cucumber–peeled and cut into chunks
2 stalks	celery–cut into chunks
1 small to medium-sized onion–peeled and cut into eights	
2 small cloves	garlic–peeled and cut into 4 pieces each
1/4 cup (plus or minus) fresh cilantro–chopped	
1 (12-ounce) can	tomato juice
4 Tablespoons	tomato purée
1/4 teaspoon	dried savory
1/4 teaspoon	dried thyme
2 Tablespoons	white vinegar
1/4 teaspoon (plus or minus) Tabasco sauce	
kosher salt and freshly ground black pepper to taste	
flavored croutons for garnish	

METHOD

1. Wash and prepare the tomatoes, pepper, cucumber, celery, onion and garlic.
2. Add 1/2 of all the vegetables and cilantro to the bowl of a food processor along with 1/2 the tomato juice, 1/2 the tomato purée, and all of the savory, thyme, vinegar and Tabasco sauce. Turn on the processor and pulse until the vegetables are finely chopped but not puréed.
3. Pour this mix into a large bowl, place the remaining ingredients into the bowl of the processor and repeat as in #2.
4. Combine this batch with the first. Mix them together and add the salt and pepper to taste. Cover the bowl with plastic wrap and refrigerate until well chilled.
5. Ladle the soup into individual soup plates, top with several croutons each and serve.

NOTES

One of the most nutritious soups you can make, this preparation is the perfect starter for a summertime dinner. It can be kept in the refrigerator for several days.

NUTRIENTS PER SERVING

CAL	PROT	CARBO	T FAT	SAT. FAT	CAL FROM FAT	CHOL	FIBER	SOD
47	1G	11G	‹1G	‹1G	5%	‹1MG	2G	203MG

Lentil Soup

Serves 6

INGREDIENTS

1 Tablespoon	olive oil
1	carrot–peeled and cut into 1-inch pieces
1 stalk	celery–cut into 1-inch pieces
4	shallots–peeled and quartered
2 (32-ounce)	cartons nonfat chicken or vegetable broth
5 small	red potatoes–peeled and quartered
2 cups	French green lentils
1/8 teaspoon (plus or minus) red pepper flakes	
4 Tablespoons	nonhydrogenated butter substitute
kosher salt and freshly ground black pepper to taste	
white truffle oil (optional but strongly recommended)	

NOTES

Bursting with protein and fiber, this heart-healthy soup, served with a salad of crunchy greens and a slice or 2 of hot sourdough bread, takes the chill out of any cold or rainy day. Because the lentils absorb liquid as they cook, it is usually necessary to add extra broth to the pot during the cooking process if the soup appears to become too thickened. White truffle oil is available in specialty grocery markets. It is wise to purchase it in the smallest amount possible as it is prone to spoilage over a shorter period of time than other oils.

METHOD

1. Coat the bottom of a large stockpot with 1 Tablespoon olive oil and heat.
2. Add the carrot, celery and shallots and "sweat" the vegetables over medium heat until the shallots soften and turn yellow.
3. Place the broth, potatoes, lentils and red pepper flakes in the pot, turn the heat to high and bring the liquid to a boil.
4. Then turn the heat down to a point where the liquid gently simmers.
5. Continue cooking at a simmer for 1 to 1 1/2 hours until the lentils become soft.
6. Remove the pot from the heat and allow the soup to cool for at least 10 minutes. Add extra broth if the soup seems too thick.
7. Working in batches, add the soup to a blender or food processor and purée.
8. Transfer the puréed soup to a clean pot, add the butter substitute and salt and pepper to taste and heat.
9. To serve, ladle the hot soup into individual bowls and swirl 1 teaspoon white truffle oil over the top of each serving.

NUTRIENTS PER SERVING

CAL	PROT	CARBO	T FAT	SAT. FAT	CAL FROM FAT	CHOL	FIBER	SOD
360	20G	53G	8G	2G	21%	0MG	11G	893MG

Gingered Butternut Squash Soup

Serves 6

INGREDIENTS

3 pounds	butternut squash (approximately 2 medium-sized)–cut in half
2 teaspoons	fresh garlic–chopped
2 teaspoons	fresh gingerroot–peeled and chopped
1 medium	onion–peeled and chopped
1	carrot–peeled and chopped
1 large	russet potato–peeled and cubed
1 (32-ounce) carton fat-free chicken broth	
kosher salt and freshly ground white pepper to taste	

NOTES

It is possible to prepare this soup ahead of time and store it in the refrigerator. Using freshly ground white pepper in place of the black allows the uniformity of the soup color to be left undisturbed. The squash may also be prepared by placing it in a steamer and cooking it on top of the stove until it is tender when pierced with a fork.

NUTRIENTS PER SERVING

CAL	PROT	CARBO	T FAT	SAT. FAT	CAL FROM FAT	CHOL	FIBER	SOD
131	5G	32G	<1G	<1G	1%	0MG	8G	299MG

METHOD

1. Preheat the oven to 350 degrees.
2. Line a baking pan with aluminum foil and lightly coat it with cooking spray.
3. Cut each squash in half and place each half face down on the foil.
4. Cover the squash with another piece of aluminum foil, place the pan in the oven and bake the squash approximately 50 minutes until the flesh of the squash is soft and easily pierced with a fork.
5. When done, let the squash cool, remove the skin and seeds and cut the squash into small cubes.
6. Coat the bottom of a nonstick pot with olive oil cooking spray (or 1 teaspoon olive oil).
7. Add the garlic and ginger, turn the heat to low and "sweat" the mix until it begins to soften.
8. Place the onion, carrot and potato in the pot and continue "sweating" until all of the vegetables begin to soften. Add 3 to 4 Tablespoons of the chicken broth to the vegetables if they start to dry out during this process.
9. Add the chicken broth to #8, bring it to a boil, lower the heat and simmer until the vegetables are soft. Add the salt and pepper to taste.
10. Remove the soup from the heat, add the chunks of cooked squash and allow the soup to cool enough to be added—a little at a time—to a food processor. Purée each batch in the processor and mix them all together in a deep stockpot.
11. Heat the soup and serve it in individual bowls.

French Fish Soup

Serves 8

INGREDIENTS FOR SOUP

4 large	onions—coarsely chopped
1/2 rib	celery—coarsely chopped
1 large bunch	fresh parsley stems—coarsely chopped
3 large	shallots—coarsely chopped
4 stalks	fresh fennel—coarsely chopped
1/2 small	carrot—peeled and coarsely chopped
2 HEADS	garlic—separate into cloves but leave skin on
2 cups	white wine
3 to 4 quarts	water
5 pounds	fish bones with heads (salmon, rockfish, bluefish, etc.)
shells from 2 pounds of shrimp	
1 1/2 cups	tomato purée
1 generous teaspoon fennel seeds	
1 Tablespoon	dried basil
1 teaspoon	dried thyme
2	bay leaves
small piece	orange rind
1/8 teaspoon (plus or minus) saffron threads—crushed	
kosher salt and freshly ground black pepper to taste	

METHOD

1. Coat a large, deep stockpot with cooking spray. Add the onions, celery, parsley, shallots, fennel and carrot and "sweat" the vegetables on low heat until they begin to soften.
2. Place each clove of garlic on a hard surface and, with the bottom of a pot or the head of a hammer, hit it so that the skin splits open. Add all of the skin-on garlic to #1.
3. Add the wine to the stockpot, raise the heat and let the liquid boil until the wine is reduced by half.
4. Next add the water, fish bones, shrimp shells, tomato purée, fennel seeds, basil, thyme, bay leaves and orange rind to the pot and simmer, uncovered, for 35 minutes.
5. Crumble the saffron into the soup and simmer for an additional 15 minutes.
6. Strain off and discard all solids, return the soup stock to the pot and add salt and pepper to taste.
7. Bring the stock to a rolling boil, ladle portions into individual bowls and serve immediately.

NOTES

When serving, place several garlic-flavored croutons topped with a bit of freshly grated Parmesan cheese on the top of each portion. The soup, a specialty of the south of France, may be frozen for up to 4 months. This preparation may require the addition of more than 1 Tablespoon of salt to bring out the best of its flavors. It is important that the salt be added cautiously in small amounts. Most markets with fresh fish departments will save bones if given a little advance notice. The flavor imparted by the shrimp shells is a vital element in this preparation. It is possible to either accumulate and freeze shells left over from other shrimp recipes or to simply include 1/2 pound of shell-on raw shrimp when making the stock. The addition of seafood and/or chunks of fish cooked in the hot broth turns this starter dish into a "main event."

NUTRIENTS PER SERVING

CAL	PROT	CARBO	T FAT	SAT. FAT	CAL FROM FAT	CHOL	FIBER	SOD
135	4G	22G	1G	‹1G	3%	0MG	7G	262MG

NUTRITIONAL INFORMATION DOES NOT INCLUDE FISH BONES AND SHRIMP SHELLS.

Croutons for Fish Soup

Serves 6

INGREDIENTS

1 large clove	fresh garlic–pressed
3 Tablespoons	olive oil
1 mini baguette	loaf of sourdough bread
2 Tablespoons	grated Parmesan cheese

NOTES

Though made from refined carbohydrate, the souring agent present in this type of bread works to lower the rate at which the body digests it. This in turn limits the ability of the carbohydrate to spike insulin levels. In addition to placing 2 to 3 croutons on top of a steaming plate of fish soup, they may be broken into pieces and used as salad croutons or as a garnish for individual servings of chilled gazpacho (see recipe page 44).

METHOD

1. Combine the garlic and oil in small dish.
2. Cut the bread on the diagonal into slices $1/4$ inch thick.
3. Spread a thin layer of the oil and garlic mix on top of each piece of bread.
4. Sprinkle a light coating of Parmesan cheese over the top of each piece of bread.
5. Bake the slices in a 350-degree oven or toaster oven until the bread is crisp and browned.
6. Cool the croutons and set them aside until ready to use.

NUTRIENTS PER SERVING

CAL	PROT	CARBO	T FAT	SAT. FAT	CAL FROM FAT	CHOL	FIBER	SOD
84	1G	3G	7G	1G	78%	1MG	‹1G	67MG

Fish Stock

Serves 6

INGREDIENTS

3 pounds	fish bones—body or heads
2 quarts	cold water
1 cup	white wine
1 medium to large	onion—finely chopped
1 stalk	celery—finely chopped
1	carrot—peeled and finely chopped
1 leek	(white only)—very well washed and thinly sliced
4 sprigs	parsley
4 whole	black peppercorns
1 whole clove	garlic—peeled and slit in 2 or 3 places
1	bay leaf
1/2 teaspoon	dried thyme
kosher salt to taste	

METHOD

1. Combine all ingredients in a large stockpot.
2. Bring the liquid to a boil, reduce the heat and let the mix simmer for 30 minutes.
3. Turn off the heat and let the broth cool in the pot before straining off and discarding the solids.

NOTES

Fish broth is rarely available ready-made so it is wise to keep some in approximately 1-cup containers in the freezer for such recipes as Ragout of Monkfish with White Beans (see recipe page 78). It also acts as a perfect stew base when chunks of fish and/or shellfish are added to the hot broth and boiled for several minutes until all of the fish is cooked through.

NUTRIENTS PER SERVING

CAL	PROT	CARBO	T FAT	SAT. FAT	CAL FROM FAT	CHOL	FIBER	SOD
52	1G	6G	‹1G	‹1G	2%	0MG	1G	16MG

NUTRITIONAL INFORMATION DOES NOT INCLUDE FISH BONES.

Seafood Minestrone

Serves 4

INGREDIENTS

3 Tablespoons	olive oil
1	leek—washed well and diced
2 stalks	celery—washed and chopped
1	carrot—peeled and diced
1/2 cup	fresh green beans—chopped
1	zucchini—washed and diced
1 (28-ounce) can	diced tomatoes
6 cups	clam broth
1/2 cup	tubetti pasta—uncooked
12	littleneck clams—washed
12	musssels—washed
12 medium	raw shrimp—peeled and deveined
1 Tablespoon	fresh thyme
kosher salt and freshly ground black pepper to taste	

METHOD

1. Heat the olive oil in a large, deep stockpot, add the leek, celery, carrot, green beans and zucchini and sauté over medium heat for approximately 5 minutes.
2. Mix the tomatoes into #1 and cook for another 3 minutes.
3. Next stir in the clam broth and bring it to a rolling boil.
4. Add the pasta and let it cook in the boiling broth for at least 6 minutes.
5. Place the clams, mussels and shrimp in the pot along with the thyme, salt and pepper, stir the ingredients together and cook the soup for another 6 minutes before serving.

NOTES

This hearty soup may be served as a starter or may act as a main course item accompanied by a crisp green salad lightly coated in a low-fat dressing and a slice or two of fresh warm sourdough bread.

Recipe courtesy of **Executive Chef Rob Klink,** *The Oceanaire Seafood Room*

NUTRIENTS PER SERVING

CAL	PROT	CARBO	T FAT	SAT. FAT	CAL FROM FAT	CHOL	FIBER	SOD
320	22G	33G	12G	2G	33%	64MG	3G	1481MG

Moroccan-Style Soup

Serves 8

INGREDIENTS

1/2 cup	dried chick-peas
1/2 cup	dried white beans
2 medium-sized	onions–sliced
3/4 cup	celery ribs and leaves–chopped
1/2 cup	fresh parsley–chopped
2 Tablespoons	(or more to taste) fresh cilantro–chopped
2 (28-ounce) cans	chopped tomatoes–drained
1 teaspoon	ground turmeric
1 teaspoon	ground cinnamon
1/2 teaspoon	saffron threads–crushed
1/4 teaspoon	ground ginger
3/4 cup	dried lentils
2 1/2 quarts	water
kosher salt to taste	
1/2 cup	dried vermicelli broken into pieces

NOTES

In addition to dietary fiber, the beans and lentils in this good-for-you recipe are high in protein and other essential nutrients. Served with a salad and a slice of warm sourdough bread, this hearty recipe is the perfect choice for a cold weather supper. The flavor of this soup gains in intensity if made a day or two before serving. It also lends itself well to freezing.

NUTRIENTS PER SERVING

CAL	PROT	CARBO	T FAT	SAT. FAT	CAL FROM FAT	CHOL	FIBER	SOD
219	13G	42G	1G	<1G	5%	0MG	9G	560MG

METHOD

1. Wash the chick-peas and the white beans under cold running water to remove excess starch. Soak them in water overnight to soften.

2. Coat a deep stockpot with cooking spray and heat. Add the onions and, stirring occasionally, "sweat" them until they soften. Add several teaspoons of water each time the onions become dry.

3. Mix the celery, parsley, cilantro and a bit more water as needed into #2 and "sweat" the mix for 2 minutes more.

4. Stir in the tomatoes and the dried spices and cook on low heat for 10 to 15 minutes.

5. Drain the chick-peas and white beans and add them to the mix along with the lentils and 2 1/2 quarts of water.

6. Bring the soup to a boil, then lower the heat and simmer, partially covered, for 1 1/2 to 2 hours.

7. Add salt to taste.

8. Approximately 10 minutes before the soup is finished add the vermicelli to the pot.

9. If after 10 minutes the stock appears too thin, it may be thickened by mashing an extra 1/2 cup canned chick-peas and adding them to the soup with the vermicelli. Raise the heat and continue cooking the soup at a gentle boil for another 5 minutes before serving.

Shrimp Soup with Lemon Grass

Serves 6

INGREDIENTS FOR SHRIMP STOCK

2¹/₂ to 3 cups	water
2 pieces	lemon grass–cut into 2-inch lengths and smashed
1 slice	fresh gingerroot (¹/₄ inch thick)–smashed
3 to 4	dried Kaffir lime leaves
shells from 1 pound of shrimp	

INGREDIENTS FOR SOUP

3 Tablespoons	fresh lime juice
1 Tablespoon	Asian fish sauce
¹/₂ teaspoon	sugar (or sugar equivalent)
¹/₂ to 1 teaspoon	finely sliced fresh jalapeño chiles–seeds removed
¹/₄ pound	fresh shiitake mushroom caps–washed, dried and thinly sliced
¹/₂ pound	small raw shrimp–shelled, cleaned and sliced in half LENGTHWISE
¹/₄ pound	bean sprouts–washed well under cold running water and drained
2	scallions–finely chopped
2 Tablespoons	(plus or minus) freshly chopped cilantro (optional)

METHOD FOR SHRIMP STOCK

1. Place the water, lemon grass, ginger, Kaffir lime leaves, and shrimp shells in a stockpot.
2. Place the pot on the stove, turn the heat to high, and boil the liquid for 5 minutes.
3. Remove the pot from the heat, cover, and set it aside.
4. When ready to use, strain and reserve the liquid stock.

METHOD FOR SOUP

1. In deep stockpot bring the shrimp stock to a rolling boil.
2. Add the lime juice, fish sauce, sugar and chiles and mushrooms.
3. Add the raw shrimp and cook approximately 2 minutes until the shrimp are cooked through.
4. Place a portion of bean sprouts in the bottom of each soup plate. Ladle soup into each plate, top with a scattering of scallions and cilantro and serve immediately.

NOTES

Dried Kaffir lime leaves and fresh lemongrass are available in Asian and other specialty markets. Smashing the lemon grass and ginger allows these ingredients to release more of their flavor. The stock may be made ahead of time and refrigerated. A bit of hot chili oil may be added to the stock for extra spiciness. But be sure to add it carefully because once added, it cannot be taken away!

NUTRIENTS PER SERVING

CAL	PROT	CARBO	T FAT	SAT. FAT	CAL FROM FAT	CHOL	FIBER	SOD
57	8G	7G	‹1G	‹1G	6%	56MG	1G	299MG

NUTRITIONAL INFORMATION DOES NOT INCLUDE KAFFIR LIME LEAVES OR SHRIMP SHELLS.

Shrimp Ball Soup

Serves 6

INGREDIENTS

2 Tablespoons	cornstarch
1	egg white–lightly beaten
8 ounces	raw shrimp–finely chopped
6 cups	nonfat chicken broth
3 Tablespoons	dry sherry
1/4-inch slice	fresh ginger–slightly smashed
1	carrot–peeled and thinly sliced into 3-inch matchstick strips
1/4 pound	fresh Chinese snow peas–thinly sliced
1/4 pound	bean curd (tofu)–cut into small cubes
1 or 2	scallions for garnish–finely chopped

NOTES

This recipe is a healthy and particularly appealing way to warm up a cold, raw day. Steps 1 and 2 may be prepared several hours in advance. The piece of sliced ginger is used as a flavoring agent for the broth and should not be eaten.

NUTRIENTS PER SERVING

CAL	PROT	CARBO	T FAT	SAT. FAT	CAL FROM FAT	CHOL	FIBER	SOD
86	11G	6G	1G	<1G	11%	56MG	1G	700MG

METHOD

1. Place the cornstarch and egg white in a bowl and beat them together with a fork until they form a completely smooth and lump-free mixture.

2. Stir the chopped shrimp into #1, cover and refrigerate 1 hour or more.

3. When ready to cook, place the chicken broth, sherry, and ginger in a deep stockpot, turn the heat to high and boil for 2 minutes.

4. Form the chilled shrimp into balls by rolling approximately 1 teaspoon of the shrimp mix in your hands and dropping each one into the boiling stock.

5. Continue to boil the soup for 1 minute after all of the shrimp balls have been added.

6. Mix the carrot, snow peas and tofu into the hot stock and cook for another 15 to 20 seconds.

7. Ladle the soup directly into individual bowls, top each with scallions, and serve immediately.

Mains

Mains

Flank Steak

Serves 4

INGREDIENTS

6 Tablespoons	golden brown mustard
2 cloves	garlic–pressed through a garlic press
1 Tablespoon	(or more to taste) freshly ground black pepper
1 (1½-pound)	flank steak

NOTES

One of the leanest of beef steaks, this preparation is a perfect summer treat served with chopped salad (see recipe page 104) and an ear of fresh corn on the cob. It is also ideal served at room temperature as a topping for a salad of crunchy greens, tomato slices, and other vegetables of choice.

NUTRIENTS PER SERVING

CAL	PROT	CARBO	T FAT	SAT. FAT	CAL FROM FAT	CHOL	FIBER	SOD
269	30G	3G	15G	6G	50%	72MG	1G	368MG

METHOD

1. Combine the mustard, garlic and pepper and, using a pastry brush, coat both sides of the steak with the mix.
2. Heat an outside grill at least 20 minutes in advance of cooking so that it becomes as hot as possible.
3. Place the flank steak on the grill and cook approximately 4 minutes per side. Brush the steak with any of the remaining mustard mix during the grilling process.
4. When done, place the steak on a cutting board, cut thin slices on the diagonal and serve.

Grilled Pork ("Moo Yang")

Serves 4

INGREDIENTS

1 (1¼-pound)	pork tenderloin or 4 large pork chops
2 Tablespoons	fresh garlic—finely chopped
¼ cup	oyster sauce
2 Tablespoons	nonsaturated vegetable oil
¼ cup	red wine
½ teaspoon	freshly ground black pepper

NOTES

Known as "the other white meat," pork tenderloin, with the exception of chicken and turkey, is the lowest of all the meats in saturated fat content. The same recipe may be made with boneless breast of chicken by substituting white wine for the red in the marinade. Chef "Dee" Buizer suggests that this dish be served with a vegetable of choice (see recipe for broccoli with shiitake mushrooms page 109) and/or with basmati rice (see recipe for perfect basmati rice page 116). She also suggests that cooking time may vary according to the heat intensity of the grill or oven.

Recipe compliments of **Chef "Dee" Buizer,** *Sweet Basil Gourmet Thai Cuisine,* Bethesda, Maryland

NUTRIENTS PER SERVING

CAL	PROT	CARBO	T FAT	SAT. FAT	CAL FROM FAT	CHOL	FIBER	SOD
251	29G	4G	12G	3G	43%	79MG	‹1G	167MG

METHOD

1. Place the pork in a plastic ziplock bag.
2. Mix all of the rest of the ingredients together and pour them into the bag with the pork.
3. Let the meat marinate in the refrigerator at least 2 hours or even overnight.
4. Remove the pork from the bag and pour the liquid into a small bowl to have it ready for basting the meat as it cooks.
5. The pork may be cooked in two ways. The first way is to place the meat on a hot outdoor grill to cook for 15 minutes, turning and basting occasionally with the marinade. The second is to prepare the pork by setting the oven temperature at 400 degrees, laying the pork on a rack sprayed with cooking oil, placing the rack on a metal tray and cooking the meat for 30 minutes. Use the marinade to brush over the surface of the meat as it cooks in the oven.
6. If pork tenderloin is used, cut the meat on the diagonal and across the grain into ¼-inch slices and arrange them on a platter for serving. The chops do not have to be sliced and may therefore be presented as they are when cooked.

Cantonese Lettuce Burgers

Serves 6

INGREDIENTS

1 head	of iceberg or romaine lettuce—well chilled
1 pound	lean, finely ground pork tenderloin (or ground chicken breast)
1/2 cup	low-sodium soy sauce
3 Tablespoons	sugar
2 teaspoons	peanut oil
1 (8-ounce) can	baby peas—drained
6	water chestnuts—drained and chopped

NOTES

Definitely a crowd pleaser, this informal dish is easy to make and fun to serve and can be served as a starter.

EDITOR'S NOTE

In addition to the ingredients listed above, a daub of hoisin sauce spread over each lettuce leaf and a sprinkling of lightly roasted pine nuts on the top of the filling gives added dimension to this winning recipe.

Recipe courtesy of **Leonard Slatkin,** Music Director, *National Symphony Orchestra*

METHOD

1. Wash the lettuce, separate the leaves, and chill them in the refrigerator for at least 5 minutes.
2. In a small bowl combine the pork (or chicken) with the soy sauce and sugar.
3. Heat the oil in a nonstick fry pan or wok, add the pork mixture and stir-fry for several minutes until the meat is cooked through.
4. Stir the peas and water chestnuts into #3 and transfer the mix to a warm baking dish.
5. To serve, place a spoonful of the mixture in a lettuce leaf, fold the leaf like a crepe and hold it with your fingers to eat.

NUTRIENTS PER SERVING

CAL	PROT	CARBO	T FAT	SAT. FAT	CAL FROM FAT	CHOL	FIBER	SOD
251	18G	16G	13G	4G	46%	50MG	2G	848MG

Spicy Chinese Noodles

Serves 6

INGREDIENTS FOR NOODLES

1/4 pound	ground pork tenderloin
2 Tablespoons	cornstarch
4 Tablespoons	cold water
1/2 pound	fresh lomein or fresh pasta noodles
1/3 pound	fresh bean sprouts—wash well and pat dry on paper toweling
1 medium to large	cucumber—peeled and cut into thin strips approximately 3 inches long

INGREDIENTS FOR SAUCE

1 Tablespoon	hoisin sauce
1/2 Tablespoon	black bean garlic sauce
3 Tablespoons	low-sodium soy sauce
2 Tablespoons	dry sherry
1 teaspoon	sugar (or sugar substitute equivalent)
1/4 to 1/2 teaspoon	hot chili paste with garlic (add with caution—very hot stuff!)
1/2 teaspoon	sesame oil (or to taste)
1 cup	nonfat chicken broth

NOTES

This dish is wonderful served at room temperature but does not reheat well. Though pork tenderloin is the least fat of all meats, those who prefer may replace it with ground turkey breast. If black bean sauce, which is sold in Asian markets and in some general supermarkets, is not readily available, the addition of a little extra hoisin sauce may be used as a substitute. This preparation may serve as either a main or side dish.

METHOD

1. Fill a large cooking pot with water and bring the water to a boil. Then turn down the heat so that the water simmers until it is ready to be used.

2. Assemble all of the sauce ingredients in a medium-sized (4-quart) pot.

3. Cook the pork in a nonstick pan on medium heat until the meat turns white and is cooked through.

4. Blot the meat well on paper toweling to remove excess fat and moisture. Then place the pork in the pot with sauce ingredients and set it aside. (Steps 2 through 4 may be prepared ahead and refrigerated until ready for use.)

5. In a small dish or custard cup, combine the cornstarch with the cold water and set the mix aside.

6. When ready to cook, heat the sauce until it is hot but not boiling.

7. Bring the water in step #1 to a vigorous boil, add the noodles and cook them for 1 minute. Drain them well, place them in a large bowl and top them with the bean sprouts and cucumber.

8. Heat the sauce (#4) to a rolling boil and, stirring constantly, add the cornstarch and stir rapidly until the sauce reaches a slightly thickened consistency. Immediately pour the hot, thickened sauce over the noodles, mix well and serve.

NUTRIENTS PER SERVING

CAL	PROT	CARBO	T FAT	SAT. FAT	CAL FROM FAT	CHOL	FIBER	SOD
200	10G	29G	4G	1G	20%	40MG	2G	452MG

Curried Chicken Salad

Serves 8

INGREDIENTS

8	skinless, boneless chicken breasts
1	carrot–peeled and chopped into several pieces
1	celery rib–cut into several pieces
1 medium	onion–peeled
1 Tablespoon	kosher salt
1/4 cup	seedless raisins
1 1/2 cups	carrots–peeled and sliced into very thin 3-inch-long strips
3/4 teaspoon	(plus or minus) freshly grated nutmeg
1 Tablespoon	(plus or minus) curry powder
1 1/4 cups	fat-free mayonnaise dressing (or more if desired)
1/2 cup	toasted slivered or sliced almonds

METHOD

1. Place the first 5 ingredients in a stockpot, add water to cover approximately 1 inch over the chicken and bring the water to a boil. Lower the heat and simmer 20 minutes.
2. Remove the pot from the heat and let the chicken remain in the broth to cool.
3. When cool, remove the chicken and set the cooking liquid aside.
4. Cut the chicken into small chunks and place them in a large cooking bowl.
5. Add the remaining ingredients to the chicken, mix well, and chill.
6. Mound the chicken salad on top of crisp romaine lettuce leaves and serve accompanied by fresh ripe tomato wedges, cucumber slices and any other fresh vegetable of choice.

NOTES

Upon completion, if the salad appears too dry, add a bit of the cooking broth to moisten it as desired. The mayonnaise substitute used in this recipe is as good a wetting and binding agent for the salad as "real" whole egg mayonnaise. The only missing ingredient is the fat!

NUTRIENTS PER SERVING

CAL	PROT	CARBO	T FAT	SAT. FAT	CAL FROM FAT	CHOL	FIBER	SOD
253	29G	16G	8G	1G	27%	73MG	2G	1124MG

Oriental Chicken Salad

Serves 6

INGREDIENTS FOR SALAD

6	bone-in chicken breast halves–skinned, washed and dried
1 slice	fresh gingerroot (1-inch-thick)–slightly smashed with a mallet
1 small head	of iceberg lettuce–shredded
4	scallions–thinly sliced
1 small (2-ounce) package of slivered almonds–slightly toasted	
1/4 cup	sesame seeds–lightly toasted
2 cups	fried rice sticks (optional)

INGREDIENTS FOR DRESSING

3 Tablespoons	sugar
2 teaspoons	salt (or less if desired)
1/2 teaspoon	freshly ground black pepper
1/4 cup	rice vinegar
1/2 cup	vegetable oil

METHOD FOR ASSEMBLY

1. Place the chicken breasts and lightly smashed gingerroot in a stockpot.
2. Add just enough cold water to the pot to cover the chicken. Bring the water to a boil, cover the pot, lower the heat, and simmer the chicken for 30 minutes before setting it aside to cool.
3. When cool, remove the chicken, discard the ginger, and shred the chicken off the bones.
4. Place the chicken, lettuce and scallions in a large bowl and set the bowl aside.
5. To make the dressing, place the sugar, salt, ground pepper and vinegar in a small saucepan and cook over low heat until the sugar dissolves.
6. Remove the pot from the heat and, after the liquid cools, whisk the oil into it.
7. Add the dressing and the rest of the ingredients to #4, toss them gently together and serve.

NOTES

By gently smashing the gingerroot, more of its flavor is released in the cooking process. All of the Asian ingredients are available in most supermarkets. It is possible to reduce the amount of sugar by substituting artificial sweeteners for at least half or—depending on the brand of sweetener used—all of the sugar in the dressing (see source list for recommended products). Both the almonds and the sesame seeds may be dry roasted on a pan in the toaster oven or in the regular oven set at 325 degrees. Sesame seeds brown within 2 to 3 minutes and should be watched carefully because they burn quite easily. Almonds, which take a bit longer to brown, must also be monitored during the roasting process.

NUTRIENTS PER SERVING

CAL	PROT	CARBO	T FAT	SAT. FAT	CAL FROM FAT	CHOL	FIBER	SOD
435	31G	12G	30G	4G	61%	73MG	2G	849MG

Singapore Chicken Salad

Serves 6

INGREDIENTS FOR CHICKEN AND MARINADE

2 teaspoons	fresh gingerroot–peeled and minced
2 teaspoons	fresh garlic–minced
3 Tablespoons	low-sodium soy sauce
3 Tablespoons	hoisin sauce
1½ Tablespoons	white vinegar
1½ teaspoons	five-spice powder
5	boneless, skinless chicken breast halves

INGREDIENTS FOR SALAD DRESSING

½ teaspoon	Dijon mustard
1 Tablespoon	sugar (or sugar equivalent)
¾ cup	white vinegar
1 Tablespoon	low-sodium soy sauce
5 Tablespoons	olive oil

INGREDIENTS FOR SALAD

1 large head	of romaine lettuce–sliced on the diagonal into 1-inch pieces
3 stalks	of celery–sliced on the diagonal into 1-inch pieces
2 large	carrots–peeled and cut on the diagonal into 1-inch pieces
½	red bell pepper–cut into thin slices
½	yellow bell pepper–cut into thin slices

METHOD FOR CHICKEN AND MARINADE

1. Combine the garlic, ginger, soy sauce, hoisin sauce, white vinegar and five-spice powder in a deep-dish ovenproof glass pie plate.
2. Add the chicken to #1 and coat it well on both sides with the marinade.
3. Place the uncovered plate in a 350-degree oven and cook the chicken 45 minutes to one hour until it is cooked through and appears glazed.
4. When done, remove the chicken from the oven, let it cool, and cut each piece on the diagonal into 5 slices.

METHOD FOR SALAD DRESSING

1. Whisk all of the dressing ingredients together in a bowl and set it aside until ready to use.

METHOD FOR SALAD ASSEMBLY

1. On a large flat serving platter, scatter the salad ingredients in the order in which they are listed.
2. Then scatter the chicken across the top of the salad, pour the dressing evenly over all and serve.

NOTES

A slice or two of warm crusty sourdough bread is the perfect accompaniment for this salad preparation. Slicing all of the chicken and vegetables the same way is known as "character cutting." It is done to add uniformity to the dish and to give the assemblage greater eye appeal. When purchasing gingerroot, always choose young pieces that are firm to the touch and have skins that appear somewhat glossy. Leftover ginger may be stored uncovered in the refrigerator for several weeks until it looks dry and wrinkled.

NUTRIENTS PER SERVING

CAL	PROT	CARBO	T FAT	SAT. FAT	CAL FROM FAT	CHOL	FIBER	SOD
394	25G	41G	14G	2G	33%	61MG	2G	587MG

Chicken Breasts with Artichokes and Capers

Serves 4

INGREDIENTS

2 teaspoons	olive oil
1 teaspoon	nonhydrogenated butter substitute
1 medium	onion–thinly sliced
2 cloves	garlic–finely chopped
1 medium	yellow pepper–thinly sliced
1 (12-ounce) jar	marinated artichokes–drained, rinsed and coarsely chopped
2 Tablespoons	small capers–drained
kosher salt and freshly ground black pepper to taste	
1½ cups	nonfat chicken broth
4	boneless, skinless chicken breast halves
1 Tablespoon	cornstarch mixed with 2 to 3 Tablespoons cold water
4 Tablespoons	freshly chopped parsley (for garnish)
juice of ¼ lemon	

METHOD

1. Heat the olive oil and the butter substitute in a large nonstick fry pan. Add the onion and garlic and "sweat" them, stirring occasionally, until softened.

2. Add the pepper, artichokes, capers, salt and pepper and broth to #1 and bring the mix to a boil.

3. Place the chicken in the hot sauce mix, cover the pan and simmer for 20 minutes.

4. Remove the chicken to a serving platter and set it aside.

5. Bring the sauce to a rolling boil and, stirring constantly, stir in the cornstarch slowly and in a steady stream until the sauce is slightly thickened.

6. Pour the sauce over the chicken, top with parsley and a squirt of lemon juice and serve.

NOTES

Originally, this recipe called for the chicken to be coated in flour, adding unnecessary carbohydrates to the dish, and then browned in oil, which added unnecessary fats and calories. A serving of basmati rice (see recipe page 116) and a portion of fresh green beans with dill (see recipe page 110) complement this chicken preparation perfectly and make for a nutritionally well-balanced and healthy meal.

NUTRIENTS PER SERVING

CAL	PROT	CARBO	T FAT	SAT. FAT	CAL FROM FAT	CHOL	FIBER	SOD
279	32G	16G	11G	1G	34%	73MG	4G	752MG

Fragrant Chicken and Vegetable Packets

Serves 4

INGREDIENTS

4	skinless, boneless chicken breasts
4 sheets	of heavy-duty aluminum foil approximately 11 to 12 inches each
kosher salt and freshly ground black pepper to taste	
1 medium	leek (white part only)–cleaned and sliced into very thin 4-inch-long strips
1 medium	carrot–peeled and sliced into very thin 4-inch-long strips
1 medium	parsnip–peeled and sliced into very thin 4-inch-long strips
4 Tablespoons	nonhydrogenated butter substitute
1/4 cup	fresh parsley–chopped
1/2 clove	(plus or minus) garlic–minced
1 teaspoon	fresh tarragon–chopped (or 1/8 teaspoon dried and crumbled tarragon)

METHOD

1. Preheat the oven to 500 degrees.
2. Place a chicken breast on each sheet of foil. Flavor with salt and pepper to taste.
3. Then place 1/4 of the vegetables on top of each chicken breast.
4. Mix the nonhydrogenated butter substitute with the parsley, garlic and tarragon and top each packet with 1/4 of this mix.
5. Fold the foil tightly over the chicken and vegetable mix and place the packets on a heavy metal baking sheet, and bake in the oven for 20 minutes.
6. Remove from the oven, place the wrapped packets on a serving plate and provide one to each person. They should be opened carefully so that the live steam within has a chance to escape.

NOTES

The fragrance upon opening these steaming packets is simply mouthwatering. The perfect accompaniments for making a totally wellbalanced and nutritionally complete meal would be a serving of perfect basmati rice (see recipe page 116) OR a slice or two of hot, crunchy sourdough bread, AND a wonderful salad of lightly dressed mixed greens. Steps 2 through 5 may be done in advance and refrigerated for several hours prior to cooking.

NUTRIENTS PER SERVING

CAL	PROT	CARBO	T FAT	SAT. FAT	CAL FROM FAT	CHOL	FIBER	SOD
272	28G	12G	12G	3G	41%	73MG	3G	169MG

Chinese Chicken with Peanuts

Serves 4

INGREDIENTS

4	boneless, skinless chicken breast halves
1	egg white–slightly beaten
1½ Tablespoons	cornstarch
1 Tablespoon	fresh garlic–minced
1 Tablespoon	fresh gingerroot–peeled and minced
1 Tablespoon	dry sherry
1 Tablespoon	white vinegar
1 Tablespoon	sugar (or sugar equivalent)
3 Tablespoons	low-sodium soy sauce
3 Tablespoons	hoisin sauce
4	scallions–cut into very thin 3-inch-long strips
½ cup	roasted peanuts
⅛ teaspoon	(plus or minus) red pepper flakes

NOTES

This high-protein low-fat version of a Chinese classic is best when served with steaming basmati rice accompanied by the broccoli with shiitake mushrooms recipe on page 109. Steps 1 through 8 of this chicken dish may be prepared in advance so that last-minute cooking time is greatly reduced. All of the oil used in the original recipe for cooking the chicken and the garlic and ginger mix has been eliminated.

NUTRIENTS PER SERVING

CAL	PROT	CARBO	T FAT	SAT. FAT	CAL FROM FAT	CHOL	FIBER	SOD
338	34G	22G	12G	2G	32%	73MG	2G	658MG

METHOD

1. Cut the chicken into thin strips 3 inches long.
2. In a bowl, beat the cornstarch and egg white together until they form a smooth, lump-free mix.
3. Add the chicken to #2 and combine thoroughly.
4. Place the garlic and ginger in a food processor and pulse until they are finely minced. Set them aside until ready to cook.
5. In a deep bowl combine the sherry, vinegar, sugar, soy sauce and hoisin sauce. Then set this aside until ready to cook.
6. Wash and dry the scallions, cut them into very thin 3-inch-long strips, cover them with plastic wrap and refrigerate until ready to use.
7. Coat a 10-inch to 12-inch nonstick fry pan liberally with cooking spray and place the pan on a burner set on medium heat. Add the chicken and, stirring constantly with wooden spoons, cook the chicken until it turns white. Remove the chicken from the pan and set it aside.
8. Using the same pan, coat it with more cooking spray, add the garlic and ginger and "sweat" them on low heat until they are softened.
9. Return the chicken to the pan, add #5, thoroughly combine the ingredients and cook until hot.
10. Add the peanuts and the red pepper flakes, mix well, pour into a bowl, top with scallions and serve immediately.

Zesty Mediterranean Chicken

Serves 6

INGREDIENTS

½ cup	diced shallots
1 large	clove garlic—crushed through a garlic press
½ cup	dried apricots—sliced
¼ cup	raisins
½ cup	dry white wine
½ Tablespoon	grated lemon peel
¼ teaspoon	ground coriander
1½ cups	fat-free chicken broth
½ Tablespoon	drained and crushed green peppercorns
½ medium-sized	green bell pepper—cut into fine strips
kosher salt to taste	
6 large	skinless, boneless chicken breasts
1 Tablespoon	cornstarch dissolved in 3 to 4 Tablespoons water

METHOD

1. Lightly coat a deep nonstick pan with cooking spray and heat until just hot.
2. Add shallots and garlic and "sweat" them, stirring occasionally, until they soften.
3. Mix the rest of the ingredients except for the chicken and cornstarch mix into #2.
4. Place the chicken in a flat layer in an ovenproof glass dish.
5. Pour #3 evenly over the chicken, cover the dish with aluminum foil, place it in a 375-degree oven and cook for 25 minutes.
6. Remove the chicken and vegetables to a serving platter and place the sauce in a pot.
7. Bring the sauce to a rolling boil and slowly pour in the cornstarch mix, stirring constantly to prevent the liquid from forming lumps.
8. When thickened pour the sauce over the chicken and serve immediately.

NOTES

This dish goes well with basmati rice (see recipe page 116), a salad of crisp greens, and a serving of strawberry applesauce (see recipe page 121).

NUTRIENTS PER SERVING

CAL	PROT	CARBO	T FAT	SAT. FAT	CAL FROM FAT	CHOL	FIBER	SOD
258	35G	16G	4G	1G	14%	91MG	1G	256MG

Lemon Grass and Curry-Flavored Thai Chicken

Serves 4

MAIN INGREDIENTS

1 pound	boneless, skinless chicken breasts
1	raw egg white mixed with 1 Tablespoon cornstarch
4	shallots—finely chopped
2 large cloves	fresh garlic—finely chopped
1/2 pound	fresh shiitake mushrooms—discard the stems, wash and blot dry the caps, and cut them into slices approximately 1/4 inch wide
1/2 pound	fresh broccoli tops (florets)—cut into bite-sized pieces
2 to 3 Tablespoons	freshly chopped cilantro (optional for garnish)

SAUCE INGREDIENTS

1	jalapeño or serrano chile—seeded and chopped
3/4 cup	nonfat chicken broth
2 Tablespoons	fresh gingerroot—peeled and thinly sliced
1 teaspoon	fresh lime juice
2 Tablespoons	Asian fish sauce
2 teaspoons	(plus or minus) curry powder
2 stalks	lemon grass, cut into 1/4-inch slices (available fresh in most markets)
1 Tablespoon	cornstarch mixed with 3 Tablespoons cold water

NUTRIENTS PER SERVING

CAL	PROT	CARBO	T FAT	SAT. FAT	CAL FROM FAT	CHOL	FIBER	SOD
211	29G	18G	3G	1G	13%	63MG	3G	899MG

METHOD

1. Combine the first 7 sauce ingredients in a 1 1/2- to 2-quart saucepan, cover and cook the sauce on medium heat for 5 minutes. Then turn off heat and set the pot aside. (This step may be completed well in advance of assembling the recipe to allow for the maximum blending of flavors.)

2. Using a sharp, straight knife, cut the chicken into long thin strips. (This is easier to do if the chicken is very cold or slightly frozen.)

3. Crack the egg white into a large, shallow bowl and beat it slightly with a fork. Add the cornstarch and blend it into the egg white with the fork until it forms a mix that is smooth and free of lumps.

4. Add the chicken to #3 and coat it well. Cover the bowl and chill the chicken in the refrigerator if time permits.

5. Place the shallots and garlic together in a food processor and pulse them until they are finely chopped.

6. Lightly spray a 10-inch to 12-inch nonstick fry pan with cooking oil. Add the garlic and shallots and "sweat" them on low heat until they become soft. Remove them from the heat when done and set them aside in a small dish.

7. Spray more cooking oil into the same pan and heat it until it is hot but not smoking. Add the chicken to the pan and, tossing the pieces with wooden spoons, cook it until each piece turns white.

8. Add the mushrooms and broccoli florets to #6 and continue to cook, tossing all of the ingredients together.

9. Mix the shallots and garlic into #6.

10. When the vegetables begin to soften, strain the sauce into #6, turn the heat to high and continue cooking until the sauce boils rapidly.

11. Push the vegetables and chicken back to the sides of the pan, leaving the sauce in the middle. Stirring constantly, pour the water/cornstarch mix in a slow stream into the boiling sauce until it is slightly thickened.

12. Push vegetable/chicken combination into the thickened sauce and top with cilantro and serve immediately.

NOTES

This dish is wonderful served with basmati rice. One of the beauties of this Thai curry-flavored dish is that it is made without adding any of the saturated fat-laden coconut milk that is usually a standard for this type of recipe.

Mexican-Style Chicken with Olives

Serves 4

INGREDIENTS

4	skinless, boneless chicken breast halves
1 medium	onion—chopped
2 cloves	garlic—chopped
1/8 cup	dry sherry
1 Tablespoon	(plus or minus) mild or medium hot chili powder
1 teaspoon	ground cumin
1 teaspoon	dried oregano
1 (28-ounce) can	crushed tomatoes in heavy purée
1/4 cup	green olives—chopped
kosher salt and freshly ground black pepper to taste	

METHOD

1. Wash the chicken breasts and blot them dry on paper toweling.

2. Coat a 10-inch to 12-inch nonstick pan with cooking spray, add the onions and garlic and "sweat" them, stirring occasionally, on low heat until they soften.

3. Mix the sherry into #2 and continue cooking until the liquid is almost gone. Then add the chicken and the rest of the ingredients, cover the pot and simmer the mix for 25 minutes.

4. Serve immediately.

NOTES

This dish may be prepared up to two days in advance and reheated when ready to serve. It also freezes well. For a complete and well-balanced menu, try serving this dish with saffron-flavored basmati rice (see recipe page 116) and a salad of fresh greens of choice.

NUTRIENTS PER SERVING

CAL	PROT	CARBO	T FAT	SAT. FAT	CAL FROM FAT	CHOL	FIBER	SOD
242	31G	19G	5G	1G	19%	73MG	5G	602MG

Moroccan-Style Lemon Chicken

Serves 6

INGREDIENTS

3 medium-sized	onions—cut into quarters and thinly sliced
5 cloves	fresh garlic—minced
1/2 teaspoon	ground ginger
1 teaspoon	paprika
1/2 teaspoon	turmeric
1/2 teaspoon	cumin
1/4 teaspoon	saffron threads—crushed
1	cinnamon stick—broken into 3 pieces
kosher salt and freshly ground black pepper to taste	
1 large	preserved lemon—Remove and discard pulp. Cut the remaining rind into thin slivers.
6	dried apricots—cut into thin slivers
6	oil-cured black olives (optional)— cut into slivers
juice of 1/2 lemon	
1 cup	fat-free chicken broth
6 large	boneless skinless chicken breasts— washed and blotted dry
1 Tablespoon	cornstarch mixed into 3 Tablespoons water
4 Tablespoons	slivered almonds (optional)—lightly toasted

METHOD

1. Coat a deep nonstick 12-inch fry pan with cooking spray.
2. Add the onion and garlic, place the pan on the burner and "sweat" the mix on low heat, stirring occasionally, until the vegetables are softened.
3. Blend all of the spices, preserved lemon, apricots, olives, lemon juice and broth into the ingredients in the pan in step #2.
4. Next add the chicken to the pan, coat it with the sauce, cover the pan and reduce the heat so that the chicken simmers for 30 minutes.
5. When ready to serve, remove the chicken to a serving dish. Bring the sauce in the pan to a rapid boil and thicken it by adding the cornstarch and water mix to it a little at a time, stirring constantly to prevent lumps from forming. Discard the cinnamon stick.
6. Pour the thickened sauce over the chicken, top with toasted almonds and serve immediately.

NOTES

Preserved lemons are available in Middle Eastern markets, specialty markets and by mail order from specialty spice and condiment companies. If they are not readily available, an alternative might be to use roasted lemons, which are prepared by lining a large flat pan with aluminum foil, cutting a lemon into very thin slices, coating each slice with a thin layer of olive oil and a sprinkling of kosher salt, placing them flat on the pan and baking them in a 350-degree oven for at least 25 minutes, until the pieces appear somewhat dry and slightly browned. This dish is traditionally made with kalamata olives, which gives the recipe a tangier but saltier flavor. Whether using oil-cured or kalamata olives, it is advisable to wash off any extra salt before slicing. Perfectly complemented when served with basmati rice, this recipe may be made ahead and frozen.

NUTRIENTS PER SERVING

CAL	PROT	CARBO	T FAT	SAT. FAT	CAL FROM FAT	CHOL	FIBER	SOD
219	35G	9G	4G	1G	17%	91MG	1G	185MG

NUTRITIONAL INFORMATION DOES NOT INCLUDE PRESERVED LEMON.

Thai Turkey Salad (Larb Gai)

Serves 4

INGREDIENTS

2 stems	fresh lemon grass (available in most markets)
10 Tablespoons	water
1⅓ pounds	ground turkey breast
4 Tablespoons	Thai fish sauce (available in most markets)
8 Tablespoons	fresh lime juice
1 teaspoon	(plus or minus) finely ground hot, dry roasted chiles
2	scallions—thinly sliced
4 Tablespoons	(plus or minus) fresh coriander (cilantro)—chopped
4 Tablespoons	(plus or minus) fresh mint—chopped
1 medium-sized	red onion—thinly sliced
1	red bell pepper—thinly sliced
1 large head	romaine lettuce
2 to 3 Tablespoons	sticky rice (optional—see recipe below)

METHOD

1. Finely slice lemon grass.
2. Place the sliced lemon grass and the water in a small covered pot and boil for 1 minute. Remove the pot from the heat and allow the lemon grass to steep several minutes after boiling.
3. Strain the water into a large nonstick fry pan and discard the lemon grass.
4. Add the turkey to #3 and stir-fry it until it is cooked through. (Most of the water will evaporate in the process.)
5. When cool, place the turkey in a large bowl, add all of the other ingredients, and mix them together well. (May be prepared several hours ahead and refrigerated until ready to use.)
6. To serve, place a spoonful of the turkey mix in the center of a large leaf of romaine lettuce. Then wrap the leaf around the mix to form an envelope-like enclosure.

NOTES

Eating this dish is a bit messy—but fun! To avoid the messy part, serve the salad on a platter of shredded iceberg lettuce accompanied by cucumber slices. Always wear rubber gloves when working with or seeding hot chile peppers. Traditionally a rice preparation called sticky rice is mixed into the salad to give it an extra-crunchy texture. The rice is made by placing 2 to 3 Tablespoons of basmati rice on a flat metal pan, baking it in a 325-degree oven until the rice browns, and then, when cool, pulsing the rice in a food processor until it is coarsely ground.

NUTRIENTS PER SERVING

CAL	PROT	CARBO	T FAT	SAT. FAT	CAL FROM FAT	CHOL	FIBER	SOD
187	31G	15G	2G	<1G	7%	70MG	3G	1455MG

Roast Breast of Turkey with Lemon and Thyme

Serves 6

MAIN INGREDIENT

1 (1½- to 3-pound) fresh bone-in turkey breast—
washed and blotted dry

INGREDIENTS FOR MARINADE

2 Tablespoons	olive oil
2 large cloves	fresh garlic—peeled and minced
1½ Tablespoons	fresh thyme—minced (or 2 teaspoons dried thyme—crumbled)
kosher salt and freshly ground black pepper to taste	

INGREDIENTS FOR SAUCE

1½ cups	unsalted chicken stock
2½ (or to taste) Tablespoons lemon juice—freshly squeezed	
kosher salt and freshly ground black pepper to taste	
¼ stick	chilled unsalted butter
4 to 6	fresh thyme sprigs for garnish (optional)

NOTES

This wonderful preparation, which transcends the seasons, is complemented by many of the "sides" in this book including strawberry applesauce (see recipe page 121), green beans with dill (see recipe page 110), and sweet pepper bouquet (see recipe page 111). It may also be accompanied with the wild rice with cranberries dish (see recipe page 117).

EDITOR'S NOTE

Nonhydrogenated butter substitute may be used, if desired, as a substitute for the butter in this recipe.

Recipe courtesy of **Michel Richard**, *Citronelle*.

NUTRIENTS PER SERVING

CAL	PROT	CARBO	T FAT	SAT. FAT	CAL FROM FAT	CHOL	FIBER	SOD
409	49G	2G	22G	6G	49%	134MG	‹1G	152MG

METHOD

1. Rub the turkey breast on both sides with the oil, pressed garlic, thyme and salt and pepper to taste.
2. Wrap the breast securely with plastic wrap and refrigerate it for at least 4 hours or overnight.
3. Place the chicken stock in a 1- to 2-quart saucepan and boil the liquid until it is reduced by half. Add the lemon juice, season with salt and pepper to taste and set sauce aside until ready to use.
4. Remove the turkey from the refrigerator, and season it again with salt and pepper. Place it on a rack set in a heatproof roasting pan and roast 1 to 1½ hours at 350 degrees until the thickest center portion registers 150 degrees F on a meat thermometer.
5. When done, remove the turkey from the oven and let it rest 30 minutes before carving.
6. Pour the sauce base (step #3) into the turkey roasting pan, set the pan on a burner, bring the liquid to a boil and stir until all browned bits are dislodged.
7. Strain the liquid through a fine sieve back into the saucepan, pressing the solid bits to extract all of their flavor.
8. Carve the turkey into thin diagonal slices and overlap the slices on 4 to 6 individual dinner plates.
9. Bring the sauce to a boil, quickly whisk in the butter, immediately remove the sauce from the heat and ladle some over the turkey on each plate.
10. If desired, garnish each with a sprig of fresh thyme before serving.

Hearty Turkey Chili

Serves 15

INGREDIENTS

4 pounds	ground breast of turkey
12 cloves	fresh garlic–minced
6 medium-sized	yellow onions–coarsely chopped
3 (16-ounce) cans	red kidney beans–drained and washed
2	red bell peppers–washed, seeded and coarsely chopped
3 (28-ounce) cans	crushed tomatoes in purée
2 (6-ounce) cans	tomato paste
3/4 cup	white vinegar
7 Tablespoons	hot Mexican-style chili powder
5 Tablespoons	ground cumin
2 Tablespoons	freshly ground black pepper
4	bay leaves

NOTES

This dish, bursting with protein and fiber, is worth making in this large amount because it freezes well in individual portions of 1 1/2 cups. If desired, top each portion with a dollop of low-fat sour cream before serving.

NUTRIENTS PER SERVING

CAL	PROT	CARBO	T FAT	SAT. FAT	CAL FROM FAT	CHOL	FIBER	SOD
325	32G	48G	3G	‹1G	7%	56MG	10G	800MG

METHOD

1. Coat a 12-inch nonstick frying pan with cooking spray.
2. Place 1/2 of the ground turkey in the pan and, using wooden spoons, cook the turkey over medium heat until no pink remains. Stir well to break the turkey into small pieces as it cooks.
3. Remove the cooked turkey to a bowl. Repeat steps 1 and 2 with the remaining uncooked turkey and, when done, add it to the turkey in the bowl.
4. Coat the bottom of an 8-quart pot with cooking spray.
5. Add the garlic and onion to the pot and "sweat" them, stirring occasionally, on low heat until softened. (Add 2 to 3 Tablespoons of water to the mix if it appears to dry out during the "seating" process.)
6. Place the cooked turkey and all of the rest of the ingredients in the pot, mix well, and heat to boiling.
7. Cover the pot, reduce the heat, and simmer the mix, stirring occasionally, for 1 hour.
8. Ladle the chili into individual soup bowls, taking care to remove the inedible bay leaves before serving.

Cornish Game Hens in Mandarin Orange Sauce

Serves 4

INGREDIENTS

4	Cornish game hens—washed and dried
⅙ recipe	Wild Rice with Cranberries per bird (see recipe page 117)
1 (11-ounce) can	mandarin oranges
1 cup	white wine

NOTES

This elegant dish is best served with a salad of delicate and interesting mixed greens lightly dressed with olive oil and balsamic vinegar and a vegetable preparation such as green beans with dill (see recipe page 110).

EDITOR'S NOTE

If any of the marinade remains after cooking, place it in a pot to heat and serve it as a sauce for the hens.

Recipe courtesy of **Michael Kaiser,** President, *The John F. Kennedy Center for the Performing Arts.*

METHOD

1. Preheat the oven to 350 degrees.
2. Stuff the cavity of each bird with an ample portion of wild rice with cranberries (see recipe page 118).
3. Place the cleaned hens on an ovenproof roasting pan lined with heavy-duty aluminum foil.
4. Combine the liquid from the oranges with the white wine to form a marinade. Lightly brush the hens with this liquid and set them in the oven to roast.
5. Baste the hens with the marinade every 10 minutes as they roast.
6. After one hour, place the mandarin orange sections on the hens and continue roasting for another 15 minutes.
7. Remove the hens from the oven and serve immediately.

NUTRIENTS PER SERVING

CAL	PROT	CARBO	T FAT	SAT. FAT	CAL FROM FAT	CHOL	FIBER	SOD
1081	74G	42G	63G	16G	53%	401MG	3G	1145MG

Zesty Gumbo

Serves 6

INGREDIENTS

1 medium	onion—chopped
2 Tablespoons	(plus or minus) fresh garlic—chopped
4	scallions—thinly sliced
1 large	green bell pepper—diced
1 (28-ounce) can	crushed tomatoes in purée
2 to 3 cups	fat-free chicken broth
1 pound	frozen okra—cut into 1/2-inch pieces
4	bay leaves
1 teaspoon	(plus or minus) Tabasco sauce
1 Tablespoon	(or more to taste) of EACH of the following: dried basil, dried oregano and dried thyme
1/2 pound	turkey chorizo, turkey andouille, or turkey kielbasa sausage—very thinly sliced
kosher salt and freshly ground black pepper to taste	
3/4 pound	thick white fish (halibut, grouper, etc.)—washed, blotted dry and cut into cubes
3/4 pound	raw shrimp—shelled, cut in half lengthwise and cleaned
3/4 pound	squid—cleaned and sliced into 3/4-inch pieces

NOTES

The okra is the only thickening agent needed for the gumbo. You can prepare steps 1 through 5 in advance and refrigerate when cool for up to two days. It is also possible to freeze the stock until ready to use.

METHOD

1. Coat the bottom of a large stockpot with cooking spray.
2. Add the onion, garlic, chopped scallions and green pepper and "sweat" them, stirring occasionally, until the vegetables soften.
3. Add the tomatoes with the purée followed by 2 1/2 cups of the broth, creating a mixture that is still fairly thick. (The other 1/2 cup of broth may be added later if the gumbo thickens too much during preparation.)
4. Mix in the okra, bay leaves, Tabasco sauce, basil, oregano, thyme, sausage and salt and pepper and simmer for 15 minutes to allow the flavors to blend.
5. Carefully adjust the seasonings for taste—you can always add but you can never take away.
6. When ready to serve, heat the broth until it is gently boiling.
7. Stir in the fish and continue cooking at a gentle boil for 5 minutes.
8. Then mix in the shrimp and squid and cook 2 to 3 minutes more.
9. Remove the bay leaves, ladle the gumbo into large soup bowls and serve accompanied by slices of hot, crusty sourdough bread, and a salad of crunchy romaine lettuce lightly coated with reduced-fat Caesar dressing.

NUTRIENTS PER SERVING

CAL	PROT	CARBO	T FAT	SAT. FAT	CAL FROM FAT	CHOL	FIBER	SOD
274	37G	24G	5G	1G	15%	213MG	5G	798MG

Photograph for this recipe appears on page 54.

Snappy Catfish

Serves 4

INGREDIENTS

1/4 cup	nonfat milk
1 Tablespoon	(or more) fresh gingerroot–peeled and finely grated
1/4 cup	finely crushed plain bread crumbs
4	catfish fillets 1/2 pound each–washed and dried
2 Tablespoons	nonhydrogenated butter substitute
1/3 cup	slivered almonds (or more if desired)
1	lemon–cut into quarters

METHOD

1. Preheat the oven to 450 degrees.
2. Coat a rectangular baking dish with cooking spray and set it aside.
3. Pour the milk into a wide shallow bowl.
4. Thoroughly mix the ginger and bread crumbs in another wide shallow bowl.
5. Dip each piece of fish in the milk and then into the bread crumb mix.
6. Place each of the well-coated pieces on the flat surface of the baking pan.
7. Dot each piece with the butter substitute and a sprinkling of almonds.
8. Place the dish in the preheated oven and bake at least 10 minutes.
9. When done, place the fish on a platter accompanied by the lemon quarters and serve immediately.

NOTES

The combination of the catfish with the other ingredients in this recipe makes for a uniquely rich-tasting dish of almost creamy consistency. Perfect accompaniments for this dish might be a salad of an interesting mix of greens, and a serving of slightly crunchy steamed green beans with fresh dill (see recipe page 110). Because the fish is coated with bread crumbs that are high in carbohydrates, it is best to avoid serving another carbohydrate item such as bread, rice or potato with this dish.

NUTRIENTS PER SERVING

CAL	PROT	CARBO	T FAT	SAT. FAT	CAL FROM FAT	CHOL	FIBER	SOD
364	44G	11G	16G	3G	40%	105MG	3G	306MG

Steamed Ginger Halibut with Papaya Slaw

Serves 6

INGREDIENTS FOR PAPAYA SLAW

1 pound	green UNRIPE papayas
3	pickled Thai chiles–chopped
1 clove	fresh garlic–pressed through a garlic press
1/4 cup	fresh lime juice
2 teaspoons	Vietnamese fish sauce
4 Tablespoons	light brown sugar
1 bunch	cilantro–washed and roughly chopped

INGREDIENTS FOR FISH

1 Tablespoon	fresh gingerroot–peeled and grated
2	shallots–peeled and thinly sliced
1 cup	white wine
6 (5-ounce) pieces	fresh boneless halibut
kosher salt and freshly ground pepper–1/8 teaspoon of each	
juice of 1/2 lime	

METHOD FOR SLAW

1. Julienne the papaya and place it in a stainless steel or glass bowl.
2. Mix all of the other ingredients—except for 1/2 the cilantro—into the papaya and let stand for 30 minutes before serving.

METHOD FOR FISH

1. Place the ginger, shallots and wine in a sauté pan and bring the mix to a simmer.
2. Sprinkle the fish with salt and pepper, carefully slip it into the simmering liquid in the pan and cover the pan loosely.
3. Simmer for 8 to 10 minutes or until the fish is firm and the flesh is opaque.

ASSEMBLY

1. Place the papaya slaw on a platter and, using a spatula, move the fish to the top of the slaw.
2. Sprinkle the juice of 1/2 lime and scatter the remaining cilantro over the fish and serve immediately.

NOTES

The combination of the tangy slaw and the sweet-fleshed fish makes for a tasty and nutritionally well-balanced meal. High quality fish sauce, pickled Thai chiles and large long papayas can be found in most Asian markets.

Recipe courtesy of **Susan Gage Caterers**, Oxen Hill, Maryland.

NUTRIENTS PER SERVING

CAL	PROT	CARBO	T FAT	SAT. FAT	CAL FROM FAT	CHOL	FIBER	SOD
251	30G	18G	3G	‹1G	12%	45MG	2G	506MG

Ragout of Monkfish with White Beans

Serves 6

INGREDIENTS

2 pounds	monkfish (or other firm fresh white fish)
2 Tablespoons	olive oil
1/2 cup	onion–chopped
1/2 cup	fresh fennel–chopped
3 cloves	fresh garlic–minced
1 cup	dry white wine
1 cup	fish stock
1/8 teaspoon	saffron
1	bay leaf–broken into 2 pieces to release its flavor (try to remove before serving as bay leaves are inedible)
2 or more sprigs	fresh thyme
1 1/2 cups	cooked white beans
1 cup	tomato pulp (fresh or canned)–skinned, seeded and chopped
1 teaspoon	lemon juice
kosher salt and freshly ground black pepper to taste	
2 Tablespoons	bread crumbs–plain or seasoned
1 Tablespoon	(plus or minus) fresh parsley–chopped

METHOD

1. Preheat the oven to 400 degrees.
2. Wash and dry monkfish, cut into 2-inch chunks and set it aside.
3. Heat 1 Tablespoon olive oil in a deep 3-quart ovenproof casserole, add the onion, fennel and garlic and "sweat" them, stirring occasionally, until they become soft and tender.
4. Stir the wine, stock, saffron, bay leaf and thyme into #3 and simmer the mix for 10 minutes.
5. Add the beans, tomato pulp, lemon juice, salt and pepper and stir to combine.
6. Tuck chunks of fish well into the mixture.
7. Moisten bread crumbs with 1 Tablespoon olive oil and sprinkle them over the top of the mix.
8. Place the uncovered casserole in the oven and bake 20 minutes.
9. Remove from the oven, sprinkle parsley over the top and serve.

NOTES

A green salad and a slice or two of hot crunchy sourdough bread for dunking makes the perfect accompaniment for this flavorful stew. If monkfish is not available , any firm, mild white fish may be substituted.

NUTRIENTS PER SERVING

CAL	PROT	CARBO	T FAT	SAT. FAT	CAL FROM FAT	CHOL	FIBER	SOD
296	32G	18G	8G	2G	24%	44MG	4G	131MG

Sesame-Crusted Salmon

Serves 4

INGREDIENTS

4 (1/2-pound)	fresh skinless salmon fillets OR one whole large 1 1/2- to 2-pound fresh skinless salmon fillet
1/2 cup	mirin (Japanese rice wine)
1/2 cup	reduced-sodium soy sauce
3/4 cup	sesame seeds
kosher salt and freshly ground black pepper to taste	

NOTES

An easy, good-for-you dish, this is a recipe that tastes as special at room temperature as it does when served hot. If served at room temperature, this dish is perfect accompanied by Asian coleslaw (see page 103). When serving the salmon hot, basmati rice and/or stir-fried broccoli or baby bok choy with fresh shiitake mushrooms (see recipe page 109) make for a winning, delicious and well-balanced meal.

NUTRIENTS PER SERVING

CAL	PROT	CARBO	T FAT	SAT. FAT	CAL FROM FAT	CHOL	FIBER	SOD
668	62G	16G	36G	6G	49%	164MG	0G	1146MG

METHOD

1. Wash the fish and blot it dry with paper toweling.
2. Place the fish, mirin and soy sauce in a ziplock plastic bag and allow the ingredients to marinate in the refrigerator for 1 to 4 hours.
3. When to ready to cook, preheat the oven to 400 degrees.
4. Spread the sesame seeds on a flat plate.
5. Remove the salmon from the marinade and set the marinade aside.
6. Season both sides of the salmon with salt and pepper.
7. Press both sides of the salmon firmly into the sesame seeds so that they will adhere well to the fish.
8. Line a broiler pan with foil. Coat a cooking rack with a liberal amount of cooking spray and place it over the pan.
9. Set the salmon on the rack, place it in the oven and cook it in the preheated oven for 12 minutes.
10. Turn the heat to broil, coat the surface of the salmon with additional marinade and, watching carefully, broil the salmon until it starts to brown.
11. Remove the salmon from the oven, transfer it to a platter and serve.

Lemon-Soaked Salmon

Serves 4

INGREDIENTS

1 pound	fresh Atlantic salmon fillet—cut into 4 pieces
1 teaspoon	lemon grass—chopped
1 Tablespoon	fresh cilantro—chopped
1 teaspoon	fresh gingerroot—peeled and chopped
2 Tablespoons	lemon juice
2 Tablespoons	honey
kosher salt and freshly ground black pepper to taste	

NOTES

This is a unique and easy-to-make rendition of heart-healthy salmon.

Recipe courtesy of **Executive Chef Morou,** *Signitures*

NUTRIENTS PER SERVING

CAL	PROT	CARBO	T FAT	SAT. FAT	CAL FROM FAT	CHOL	FIBER	SOD
219	26G	10G	8G	1G	34%	72MG	<1G	57MG

METHOD

1. Preheat the oven to 350 degrees.
2. Place the salmon fillets in a ziplock plastic bag.
3. Combine the rest of the ingredients and add them to #2.
4. Chill the marinating salmon in the refrigerator for at least 1/2 hour.
5. When ready to cook, remove the salmon from the marinade, dry it with a paper towel and season each piece with salt and pepper.
6. Heat the oil in an ovenproof sauté pan and sear the salmon skin side up for 3 minutes.
7. Transfer the salmon in the pan into a 350-degree oven and cook for approximately 5 minutes or until it reaches the desired degree of doneness.
8. Arrange each piece of salmon on an individual plate and serve accompanied by a portion of the tomato sauce on page 81.

Tomato Sauce

Serves 4

INGREDIENTS

5	plum tomatoes–roasted
1	red pepper–roasted
1 medium	onion–roasted
5 cloves	garlic–roasted
1/4	mango–chopped
1/4 fresh	pineapple–chopped
1/4	apple–chopped
1 cup	pineapple juice
1 teaspoon	ground cumin
1 Tablespoon	olive oil
1 Tablespoon	fresh cilantro–chopped
1 teaspoon	fresh lime juice
kosher salt, freshly ground black pepper and sugar to taste	

METHOD

1. Purée the tomatoes, pepper, onion, garlic, mango, pineapple and apple in a food processor.
2. With the blade still running, carefully add the pineapple juice and the cumin and blend until the purée is smooth.
3. Heat the oil in a saucepan, add #2 to the pan and cook for 3 minutes on medium heat.
4. Remove the mix from the heat, season with the cilantro, lime juice, salt, pepper, and sugar and serve hot.

NOTES

This tangy sauce with its unusual combination of ingredients is the perfect foil for the Lemon-Soaked Salmon recipe on page 80. It also acts as a complement for most other grilled fish preparations.

Recipe courtesy of **Executive Chef Morou,** *Signitures*

NUTRIENTS PER SERVING

CAL	PROT	CARBO	T FAT	SAT. FAT	CAL FROM FAT	CHOL	FIBER	SOD
134	2G	25G	4G	1G	25%	0MG	3G	10MG

Succulent Salmon

Serves 4

INGREDIENTS

6 Tablespoons	low-sodium soy sauce
4 Tablespoons	honey
1 Tablespoon	sugar
2½ Tablespoons	(or to taste) Dijon mustard
1 (2-pound)	salmon fillet with skin left on the bottom – wash and pat dry

NOTES

This is yet another way to give a distinctive personality to salmon, a fish that contains essential, health-promoting omega-3 trans fatty acid. Almost any seasonal vegetable or salad preparation found in this book will go well with this salmon preparation.

NUTRIENTS PER SERVING

CAL	PROT	CARBO	T FAT	SAT. FAT	CAL FROM FAT	CHOL	FIBER	SOD
517	54G	25G	22G	4G	38%	164MG	‹1G	1120MG

METHOD

1. Line a 9-inch by 13-inch glass baking dish with a layer of heavy-duty foil and coat the surface of the foil lightly with cooking spray.
2. Blend the soy sauce, honey, sugar and mustard together in a bowl.
3. Pour #2 into the baking dish and place the salmon fillet SKIN SIDE UP over it. Cover the dish with plastic wrap and refrigerate for at least one hour prior to cooking.
4. Preheat the oven to 350 degrees.
5. Remove the plastic wrap, turn the salmon over so the SKIN SIDE is DOWN and place the salmon in the oven. Bake for 20 to 30 minutes.
6. Turn the oven setting to broil, and, basting frequently, let the fish cook another 2 to 3 minutes until the top of the salmon appears shiny and glazed. Serve immediately.

Grilled Salmon with Ginger

Serves 4

INGREDIENTS

1 (2-pound)	fresh salmon fillet with skin left on the bottom
1/4 cup	low-sodium soy sauce
1 teaspoon	sesame oil
3 or 4 Tablespoons	fresh gingerroot—peeled and minced
3 cloves	garlic—finely minced
4 Tablespoons	white wine
2 Tablespoons	(plus or minus) scallions—chopped
2 Tablespoons	fresh parsley—chopped
2 Tablespoons	(plus or minus) fresh dill—chopped
1 teaspoon	freshly ground black pepper

NOTES

The skin should get quite crispy during the grilling process. However, it burns easily and great care must be taken to see that it doesn't flame up and burn off. To reduce the possibility of losing the skin, the grill must be well oiled prior to cooking and rubbed well with the inside of a raw potato. Not only is the skin of the salmon a crispy treat, it also, like the fish itself, is filled with healthy and beneficial omega-3 trans fatty acid. This recipe may be adapted to indoor oven broiling. Simply raise the upper oven rack close to the flame and turn the temperature setting to broil. Place the salmon skin side up on a cooking rack that has been generously coated with cooking spray. Then place the rack on a metal pan covered with aluminum foil and follow the cooking directions as specified in step #7. This tasty fish is complemented by almost any salad or vegetable preparation in this book.

METHOD

1. Wash the salmon, pat it dry and place it in a gallon-size ziplock bag.
2. Mix the rest of the ingredients together, add them to #1, and let the fish marinate in the refrigerator several hours before cooking.
3. Coat an outdoor grill liberally with cooking spray and light the grill approximately 1/2 hour before cooking to allow it to get very hot.
4. Remove the salmon from the marinade.
5. Place the marinade in a glass bowl and brush the fish with it occasionally while cooking.
6. Cook the salmon approximately 4 to 5 minutes per side, being careful when turning the fish not to lose the skin.
7. Add a bit of water to the marinade left in the bowl, cover the bowl with plastic wrap and place it in the microwave for one to two minutes to heat. Then pour the marinade into a sauce boat and serve it as an accompaniment for the fish.

NUTRIENTS PER SERVING

CAL	PROT	CARBO	T FAT	SAT. FAT	CAL FROM FAT	CHOL	FIBER	SOD
451	53G	4G	22G	4G	45%	164MG	<1G	634MG

Grilled Salmon Sandwich

Serves 4

INGREDIENTS

12 slices	turkey bacon
1 pound	fresh boneless, skinless salmon fillet
kosher salt and freshly ground black pepper to taste	
4 whole	wheat rolls
4 large	slices tomato
4 large	leaves romaine lettuce
8 long, thin	Gherkin sandwich pickle slices

NOTES

A serving of chilled gazpacho is the perfect complement to this unique, healthy and easy summer alternative to the beef burger. Condiments such as nonfat mayonnaise spread and/or ketchup may be added as desired. If the fish is to be cooked in the oven, raise the oven rack closest to the flame and set the temperature on broil. Cover a metal pan with aluminum foil and place a rack that has been well coated in cooking spray over the pan. Place the fish on the sprayed rack and broil for approximately 4 minutes per side.

METHOD

1. Place 6 slices of turkey bacon in a glass plate, cover them with paper toweling, slip the plate in the microwave and cook the turkey bacon approximately 5 minutes or until it is crisp. When done, set the cooked pieces aside, wipe the cooking residue from the glass plate and repeat the process with the remaining batch of bacon.
2. Liberally coat the salmon fillet with salt and pepper, and cook it on a hot outdoor grill, for approximately 4 minutes on each side.
3. When done, place the salmon on a cutting board and slice it on the diagonal into 4 pieces.
4. To serve, place each piece of salmon on a roll with a slice of the tomato, a leaf of romaine lettuce, 3 slices of turkey bacon, and a slice or 2 of the pickle.

NUTRIENTS PER SERVING

CAL	PROT	CARBO	T FAT	SAT. FAT	CAL FROM FAT	CHOL	FIBER	SOD
401	35G	21G	20G	5G	44%	112MG	3G	958MG

Salmon Cakes

Serves 4

INGREDIENTS

2 Tablespoons	nonhydrogenated butter substitute
2 Tablespoons	olive oil
1/2 cup	red bell pepper–finely diced
1/2 cup	yellow bell pepper–finely diced
3/4 cup	red onion–finely diced
1 1/2 cups	celery (4 stalks)–finely diced
1/4 teaspoon	Tabasco sauce
1/2 teaspoon	Worcestershire sauce
1 1/2 teaspoons	Old Bay seasoning
3	egg whites
1	egg yolk
1 (24- to 28-ounce)	can Red Sockeye salmon–drained, cleaned of all skin and bone and flaked
1/2 cup	seasoned bread crumbs
1/2 cup	low-fat mayonnaise
2 teaspoons	Dijon mustard

NOTES

This zesty salmon preparation may be served in several ways: as a main course with salad and a vegetable, in a more informal presentation by placing it in a whole wheat bun, or by shaping the mix into small cakes and serving them as an appetizer. For a change of pace, this recipe may be made with crabmeat instead of salmon.

NUTRIENTS PER SERVING

CAL	PROT	CARBO	T FAT	SAT. FAT	CAL FROM FAT	CHOL	FIBER	SOD
661	48G	20G	45G	9G	60%	190MG	3G	1936MG

METHOD

1. Melt 1 Tablespoon nonhydrogenated butter substitute with 1 Tablespoon olive oil in a large nonstick sauté pan.
2. Add the peppers, onion, celery, Tabasco sauce, Worcestershire sauce, and Old Bay seasoning to the pan and "sweat" over low to medium heat until the vegetables are soft.
3. Remove the pot from the heat and allow the ingredients to cool to room temperature.
4. Beat the egg whites and the yolk together in a small bowl.
5. Place the salmon, bread crumbs, mayonnaise and mustard in a large bowl, add the eggs and mix the ingredients together.
6. Add the cooked vegetables to #5, cover the bowl and chill the mix in the refrigerator for 1 to 2 hours.
7. When ready to cook, preheat the oven to 350 degrees.
8. Shape the salmon mix into 4 cakes.
9. Melt the remaining nonhydrogenated butter substitute and olive oil in a nonstick pan, add the salmon cakes and sauté them on low heat until each side is slightly browned.
10. While the cakes are browning, line a baking pan with foil and coat it lightly with cooking spray.
11. Transfer the browned salmon cakes to the baking pan, place them in the oven, bake them for 1/2 hour and serve.

Steamed Salmon Steaks with Black Beans

Serves 2

INGREDIENTS

1 Tablespoon	salted black beans–rinsed, blotted dry on paper toweling and chopped
2 (1/2- pound)	fresh salmon steaks–washed and patted dry on paper toweling
2 Tablespoons	reduced-sodium soy sauce
2 Tablespoons	dry sherry
1/2 teaspoon	sesame oil
1/4 teaspoon	fresh ground black pepper
1/2 teaspoon	(plus or minus) fresh gingerroot–peeled and finely chopped
1/4 teaspoon	sugar
2	scallions–cut into 3-inch-long slivers

NOTES

Bags of dried salted black beans are available in Asian markets. They may be stored indefinitely in an airtight container and do not need to be refrigerated. Steamed basmati rice (recipe page 116) is the perfect accompaniment for this dish.

METHOD

1. Place the beans in a small sieve, and rinse them under cold running water to remove excess salt. Press the beans dry in paper toweling, then finely chop them.
2. Rinse the salmon, pat it dry and place it on a glass pie plate.
3. Combine the soy sauce, sherry, sesame oil, pepper, ginger, sugar and black beans and pour it over the fish.
4. Bring water to a boil in a steamer, set the plate with the fish and sauce in the steamer, cover, and steam for 10 minutes.
5. Transfer the fish to a serving platter, top it with the liquid left in the pie plate, scatter the scallions over the fish and serve.

NUTRIENTS PER SERVING

CAL	PROT	CARBO	T FAT	SAT. FAT	CAL FROM FAT	CHOL	FIBER	SOD
456	54G	5G	22G	4G	44%	164MG	1G	646MG

Tuna Fish Salad

Serves 2

INGREDIENTS

1 (12-ounce) can	tuna packed in water–drained and flaked
1 rib	celery–diced
juice of 1/2 lemon	
3 Tablespoons	fat-free mayonnaise dressing (or more if desired)

METHOD

1. Place the drained and flaked tuna in a bowl.
2. Add the celery, lemon juice and fat-free mayonnaise dressing to #1 and mix well.
3. Cover and refrigerate until ready to use.

NOTES

The versatility of tuna lends itself to the addition of many creative and interesting preparations. This recipe is a good standard for sandwiches and is ideal, when accompanied by fresh summer vegetables, for a hot weather salad supper.

NUTRIENTS PER SERVING

CAL	PROT	CARBO	T FAT	SAT. FAT	CAL FROM FAT	CHOL	FIBER	SOD
204	40G	5G	1G	<1G	6%	47MG	<1G	752MG

Provence-Style Tuna Salad

Serves 6

INGREDIENTS

2 (12-ounce) cans	solid white water-packed tuna–drained and flaked
3 to 4 Tablespoons	small capers–drained and chopped
1 small	red onion–thinly sliced
1 Tablespoon	(plus or minus) herbes de Provence

INGREDIENTS FOR SALAD DRESSING

2 teaspoons	anchovy paste
4 Tablespoons	lemon juice
1	fresh garlic clove–pressed
¼ cup	olive oil
2 to 3 Tablespoons	balsamic vinegar
kosher salt and freshly ground black pepper to taste	

METHOD FOR TUNA

1. Mix all of the ingredients together in a deep bowl and set aside.

METHOD FOR SALAD ASSEMBLY

1. Place all of the dressing ingredients in a small bowl and whisk them together until they are well combined.
2. Pour the dressing into the tuna, mix well and refrigerate several hours before serving to allow the flavors to integrate.

NOTES

This delightful and easy summer salad may be served over a bed of romaine lettuce accompanied by fresh ripe tomato wedges and slices of cucumber. It may also be served as a sandwich by placing each portion in a hollowed-out sourdough baguette roll with lettuce, cucumber and sliced rather than quartered tomatoes. This preparation also makes for a wonderful hors d'oeuvre when spooned onto whole wheat crackers. Herbes de Provence, a dried blend of spices, may be found in most general supermarkets.

NUTRIENTS PER SERVING

CAL	PROT	CARBO	T FAT	SAT. FAT	CAL FROM FAT	CHOL	FIBER	SOD
220	28G	4G	10G	1G	42%	32MG	‹1G	527MG

Linguini with Clam Sauce

Serves 4

INGREDIENTS

1 Tablespoon	olive oil
1 Tablespoon	nonhydrogenated butter substitute
3 cloves	garlic–finely minced
2	shallots–finely chopped
3 (6-ounce) cans	minced clams–drain and reserve liquid
8 canned	flat anchovy fillets–drained
1/2 cup	dry white wine
1/2 teaspoon	dried rosemary–crumbled
kosher salt and freshly ground black pepper to taste	
3/4 pound	whole wheat linguini
1/4 cup	fresh parsley–chopped

NOTES

Because pasta is high in carbohydrate, it is suggested that portions be limited to 3 ounces per person—even when using whole wheat pasta. It is possible to add extra clams, shrimp, or calamari to the sauce for a more filling dish. Freshly ground Parmesan cheese may be added as an aromatic and flavorful topping to each individual serving. A salad of a combination of interesting greens topped by tomato slices is the perfect accompaniment for this dish. Oven-roasted, herbed or simply steamed vegetables go well with both the pasta and the salad. It is strongly recommended that NO OTHER high carbohydrate food such as bread be eaten with this meal.

METHOD

1. Heat the olive oil and butter substitute in a 10-inch nonstick skillet. Add the garlic and shallots and "sweat" them on a low flame until they are softened. (If the vegetables become too dry, add 1 to 2 Tablespoons of the clam juice to the garlic and shallots as they cook.)

2. Add the anchovies and 2 to 3 Tablespoons of the clam juice and continue cooking until the anchovies dissolve.

3. Mix the clams, 1/2 of the remaining clam juice, the wine, rosemary, salt and pepper to taste into #2 and simmer for 15 minutes.

4. While the sauce is cooking, bring a large pot of water to a rolling boil.

5. Add the linguini to the water and continue to boil until the pasta is cooked yet still firm (or al dente).

6. Pour the linguini into a colander set in the sink. Drain the noodles well and immediately place the drained noodles in the pot with the simmering sauce. Turn up the heat, mix the sauce and noodles together and, if desired, add as much of the remaining clam juice as you wish. When hot and boiling, pour the mix into a heatproof bowl, sprinkle with parsley and serve.

NUTRIENTS PER SERVING

CAL	PROT	CARBO	T FAT	SAT. FAT	CAL FROM FAT	CHOL	FIBER	SOD
450	24G	71G	8G	1G	15%	30MG	11G	903MG

Provence-Style Shrimp Salad

Serves 4

INGREDIENTS FOR SALAD

2 (10-ounce) packages of frozen artichoke hearts–cooked until slightly tender and patted dry with paper toweling when cool	
1 large jar (15 ounces) of roasted red peppers–washed, drained and cut into slices	
4 to 6 ounces	pitted kalamata olives–washed and drained
2 cans	of hearts of palm (15 ounces each)–washed, drained and cut into 1/2-inch rounds
1 1/2 pounds	cooked shrimp–shelled and cleaned
10	cherry tomatoes–cut into halves
1 head	of romaine or Boston lettuce–separate, wash and dry the leaves

INGREDIENTS FOR MARINADE

1/4 cup	(plus or minus) balsamic vinegar
1/4 cup	olive oil
1 Tablespoon	fresh oregano–chopped (or 1 teaspoon dried oregano)
1 clove	fresh garlic–minced
kosher salt and freshly ground black pepper to taste	

METHOD FOR SALAD ASSEMBLY

1. Whisk the marinade ingredients together in a large bowl.
2. Mix all of the main salad ingredients into #1 EXCEPT for the tomatoes and lettuce.
3. Cover and refrigerate #2 at least several hours to one day in advance of use.
4. When ready to prepare, arrange the lettuce leaves on a round platter.
5. Drain the marinade off of #2 and place the shrimp mix in the center of the lettuce. Scatter the cherry tomatoes over the salad and serve.

NOTES

Because there are so few carbohydrates in this salad, a slice or two of hot crusty sourdough bread makes for a well-balanced and ideal accompaniment for this meal.

NUTRIENTS PER SERVING

CAL	PROT	CARBO	T FAT	SAT. FAT	CAL FROM FAT	CHOL	FIBER	SOD
591	47G	39G	30G	4G	44%	332MG	13G	2405MG

Garlic Shrimp

Serves 4

INGREDIENTS

2 Tablespoons	nonhydrogenated butter substitute
1/4 cup	scallions–chopped
3 teaspoons	fresh garlic–chopped
3/4 pound	medium-sized shrimp–shelled and cleaned
2 Tablespoons	(plus or minus) Creole seasoning
1 (15-ounce) can	tomato sauce
1 (12-ounce) package fresh angel hair pasta	

METHOD

1. Fill a large pot with water and heat it to boiling. Turn the heat down so that the water simmers until the pasta is ready to be cooked.
2. Melt the butter substitute in a large nonstick fry pan.
3. Add the scallions, garlic and shrimp and stir-fry on medium to high heat for 30 seconds.
4. Sprinkle the Creole seasoning over the shrimp and continue cooking for 3 to 4 minutes.
5. Stir in the tomato sauce and simmer the mix for 12 to 15 minutes.
6. Approximately 2 minutes before serving, place the pasta in the hot water, boil it for 1 minute or less and drain well.
7. Add the pasta to the pan with the hot shrimp, toss them together and serve immediately.

NOTES

Freshly ground Parmesan cheese may be added to each individual portion according to taste. A salad of crunchy romaine greens lightly dressed with low-fat Caesar dressing makes for a tasty meal.

Recipe courtesy of **Darrell Green,** former Redskins cornerback and founder of the *Darrell Green Youth Life Foundation* (DGYLF), which operates learning centers nationwide

NUTRIENTS PER SERVING

CAL	PROT	CARBO	T FAT	SAT. FAT	CAL FROM FAT	CHOL	FIBER	SOD
390	25G	56G	7G	2G	17%	188MG	5G	3617MG

Shrimp Kung Pao

Serves 4

INGREDIENTS

1½ pounds	raw shrimp
1	raw egg white
1 Tablespoon	cornstarch
¼ cup	cider vinegar
5 teaspoons	sugar (or sugar equivalent)
¼ cup	ketchup
1 Tablespoon	(plus or minus) fresh garlic–peeled and minced
1 Tablespoon	(plus or minus) fresh gingerroot–peeled and minced
4	scallions–cut on the diagonal into 1-inch pieces

NOTES

This dish is wonderful accompanied by basmati rice. However, calorie and carbohydrate watchers may use the alternative of eliminating the rice and serving the shrimp on top of shredded iceberg lettuce. Steps 1 through 5 may be prepared in advance. Preparing the garlic and ginger for use in this recipe is most easily accomplished if they are placed together in a food processor and pulsed until minced.

NUTRIENTS PER SERVING

CAL	PROT	CARBO	T FAT	SAT. FAT	CAL FROM FAT	CHOL	FIBER	SOD
190	29G	15G	1G	‹1G	7%	252MG	1G	485MG

METHOD

1. Shell, clean and slice each shrimp in half LENGTHWISE.
2. Place the egg white in a bowl and beat it slightly with a fork. Add the cornstarch to the egg white and beat them together until they form a smooth and lump-free mix.
3. Add the shrimp to #2, mix well, cover the bowl and refrigerate for 1 hour or more before cooking.
4. Combine the sauce ingredients of cider vinegar, sugar, and ketchup in a bowl and set it aside.
5. Coat a large nonstick frying pan with cooking spray. Add the garlic and ginger and "sweat" them on low heat, stirring occasionally, until they soften. Remove the ginger and garlic to a small dish and set it aside.
6. Coat the same pan with additional cooking spray, and return it to the stove to heat. Add the shrimp and toss them with wooden or plastic spoons for 3 to 5 minutes until they are just cooked through.
7. Stir the garlic, ginger and sauce mix into the shrimp and continue cooking until the mix is piping hot.
8. Transfer the shrimp to a serving dish, scatter scallions over the top and serve immediately.

Spanish-Style Shrimp

Serves 4

INGREDIENTS

1¼ pounds	shrimp
1 medium	onion–peeled and chopped
1 clove	fresh garlic–peeled and finely chopped (or pressed)
1 (28-ounce) can	crushed tomatoes in heavy purée
1 Tablespoon	(plus or minus) chili powder
½ teaspoon	sugar (or sugar equivalent)
¼ teaspoon	dried marjoram
1	bay leaf
⅛ teaspoon	cayenne
¼ cup	(plus or minus) fresh chopped cilantro (optional)

METHOD

1. Shell shrimp, cut them in half LENGTHWISE, wash and pat them dry.
2. Coat a 12-inch nonstick pan with cooking spray, add the onion and garlic and, stirring occasionally, "sweat" them on low heat until they soften.
3. Stir the tomatoes, chili powder, sugar, marjoram, bay leaf, and cayenne into #2, bring the mix to a boil and simmer for two minutes.
4. Mix in the shrimp and continue cooking until they turn pink throughout.
5. Remove and discard bay leaf. Transfer #4 to a large bowl, scatter the cilantro across the top and serve immediately.

NOTES

Cutting the shrimp lengthwise causes them to curl during the cooking process into a shape that is better for holding the sauce. Saffron basmati rice (recipe page 116) is the perfect accompaniment for this dish.

NUTRIENTS PER SERVING

CAL	PROT	CARBO	T FAT	SAT. FAT	CAL FROM FAT	CHOL	FIBER	SOD
190	26G	19G	2G	<1G	9%	210MG	5G	524MG

Scampi in Salsa di Fave Insalatine di Carciofine e Porri

Serves 4

INGREDIENTS

1 pound	baby artichokes–cleaned and cut into thin strips
1/4 bunch	leeks (tender white parts)–cleaned and cut into thin strips
2	lemons–juice only
freshly ground white pepper to taste	
1/8 teaspoon	salt
2 pounds	langoustine–unshelled
3 Tablespoons	extra-virgin olive oil
1	shallot–finely chopped
1 pound	fresh fava beans–shelled
4 leaves	fresh basil
4 slices	sourdough bread–toasted

NOTES

Perfect for a starter or a summer luncheon dish, this preparation may be made with shrimp if langoustine are not readily available.

Recipe courtesy of **Franco Nuschese,** Host of *Café Milano*

NUTRIENTS PER SERVING

CAL	PROT	CARBO	T FAT	SAT. FAT	CAL FROM FAT	CHOL	FIBER	SOD
562	50G	56G	15G	3G	24%	336MG	10G	879MG

NUTRITIONAL INFORMATION CONTAINS 1/8 TEASPOON SALT.

METHOD

1. In a bowl toss the baby artichokes and leeks in some of the lemon juice and white pepper to taste and set it aside until ready to use.

2. Heat water and a pinch of salt in a deep pot, add the langoustine and boil for 5 minutes. Drain the water and set the langoustine aside.

3. Pour 1 Tablespoon of the olive oil into a nonstick saucepan, add the shallot and, stirring constantly, cook for 2 minutes over medium heat.

4. Add the fava beans to #3 along with a bit of water and, still stirring, cook them for 5 minutes.

5. Put the cooked fava beans, fresh basil, 1 Tablespoon olive oil and a pinch of salt in a blender and process to obtain a fine green sauce.

6. Peel and discard the tails and toss the langoustine in a bowl with some of the lemon juice, a pinch of salt and 1 Tablespoon olive oil.

7. Toss the baby artichokes and leeks in some of the lemon juice and a bit of freshly ground white pepper.

8. To serve, spoon the green sauce over the bottom of a round plate, set the langoustine tails in a circle, arrange the artichoke and leek mix around the langoustine, and place the toasted bread over the salad.

Guilt-Free Egg Salad

Serves 6

INGREDIENTS

1 (8-ounce) package liquid egg substitute	
6 whole	egg whites–hard-cooked
2 medium stalks	celery–finely chopped
3 Tablespoons	fat-free mayonnaise dressing (or more if desired)
1/2 teaspoon	(plus or minus) garlic salt
freshly ground black pepper to taste	

NOTES

This preparation allows you to enjoy a favorite recipe without any fat. Garlic salt is but one of many flavoring ingredients that may be added to the basic "egg" mix. Another is to add fresh chopped tarragon, salt and pepper to taste OR to simply add a touch of curry powder along with salt and pepper to taste. It is possible to use this salad as an hors d'oeuvre with crackers or whole wheat pita slices, or to serve it as a main course by placing it on a bed of lettuce surrounded by a variety of fresh and colorful vegetables such as tomato wedges, sliced cucumbers, red, green and yellow pepper strips and carrot sticks. Nonfat mayonnaise dressing is a great substitute for fat-laden regular mayonnaise. Both are simply wetting agents that hold the egg mix together. The salad relies on the addition of herbs and seasonings to give it its taste definition.

METHOD

1. Pour the egg substitute into a bowl and beat it with a whisk.
2. Lightly coat an 8-inch to 10-inch nonstick fry pan with cooking spray and heat.
3. When hot, add the egg substitute and stir with a nonmetal spatula until it is cooked through and firm. Remove the pan from the heat and set the contents aside to cool.
4. Place the eggs in a pot and add enough cold water to cover them. Bring the water to a boil and cook the eggs for 20 minutes.
5. Remove the pot from the heat, pour off the hot water, add cold water and cool the eggs until they reach room temperature.
5. Peel the eggs, DISCARD THE YOLKS, chop the whites and place them in a bowl.
6. Chop the egg substitute and add it to #5.
7. Add the rest of the ingredients, mix well, cover and refrigerate to chill well before serving.

NUTRIENTS PER SERVING

CAL	PROT	CARBO	T FAT	SAT. FAT	CAL FROM FAT	CHOL	FIBER	SOD
43	7G	3G	‹1G	‹1G	0%	0MG	‹1G	362MG

Pasta with Spicy Caper and Shiitake Mushroom Sauce

Serves 4

INGREDIENTS

6 to 8	sun-dried tomatoes–rehydrated and sliced
10	fresh shiitake mushrooms–washed and sliced
1 large jar	(approximately 25 ounces) of ready-made low-fat Italian roasted garlic or puttanesca sauce
1 Tablespoon	small capers–chopped
1 teaspoon	crushed dried oregano
1/4 teaspoon	crushed dried thyme
1/4 teaspoon	red pepper flakes
12 ounces	fresh angel hair pasta
1/2 ounce	freshly grated Parmesan cheese
4 to 5 Tablespoons	fresh basil–coarsely chopped

NOTES

A light topping of freshly grated Parmesan cheese may be added to each individual serving. Crunchy romaine lettuce lightly coated with reduced-fat Caesar salad dressing makes the perfect salad accompaniment for this dish. Sun-dried tomatoes come in two versions. The plain dried ones must be soaked in hot water for 15 minutes in order to become reconstituted and made ready for use. Tomatoes packed in oil may be used but should be blotted well in paper toweling in order to remove excess oil. No bread of any kind should be a part of this meal because it would disturb the balance of the other components with an overload of carbohydrates.

NUTRIENTS PER SERVING

CAL	PROT	CARBO	T FAT	SAT. FAT	CAL FROM FAT	CHOL	FIBER	SOD
398	17G	72G	5G	1G	11%	65MG	9G	1055MG

METHOD

1. Bring a large pot of water to a boil. Lower the heat, cover the pot and let the water simmer until ready to use.
2. Place the sun-dried tomatoes in a small bowl, cover them with hot water, and set them aside for 15 minutes until they become softened.
3. When soft, blot them well on paper toweling, cut them into thin slices, and set them aside until ready for use.
4. Remove and discard the stems from the mushrooms.
5. Wash the mushroom caps, blot them dry with paper toweling, slice them into 1/4- to 1/2-inch-wide strips and set them aside.
6. Pour the pasta sauce into a large deep sauté pan and heat the sauce on a low to medium setting.
7. Add the capers, oregano, thyme, mushrooms, tomatoes and red pepper flakes to the sauce and simmer for 2 minutes. Then turn the heat to low, cover the pan and leave it on the burner.
8. Bring the water back to a rolling boil, add the pasta and cook it for 1 minute.
9. Drain the pasta into a colander, shake it well to remove all excess water and add the pasta to the pan containing the sauce.
10. Mix the pasta and sauce together and heat until very hot.
11. Place the mix in a large serving bowl, top with fresh Parmesan cheese and basil and serve immediately.

Vegetable Lasagna

Serves 6

INGREDIENTS

5 large	carrots—peeled and thinly sliced
2 large	zucchini—washed and thinly sliced
1 pound	fresh spinach—washed, squeezed dry in paper toweling and coarsely chopped
2 (15-ounce) containers of part-skim Ricotta cheese	
1/2 cup	liquid egg substitute (equals 2 whole eggs)
1 (12-ounce) box	of lasagna pasta noodles (enough to make 3 layers)
1 Tablespoon	dried and crumbled oregano (optional)
2 1/2 (14-ounce) bottles spicy red pepper pasta sauce	
1 (16-ounce) package shredded part-skim mozzarella cheese	

NOTES

This dish, with its carbohydrate, protein and vegetable content, is nutritionally complete and should be accompanied by nothing more than a fresh salad composed of interesting seasonal greens lightly dressed with low-fat dressing. Tomato and cucumber slices or any other raw vegetables of choice may be added to the salad according to preference. Bread should NOT be served with this preparation because it would overload the meal with carbohydrates. There are many brands of ready-made spicy red pasta sauces available in grocery markets. Be sure to read the labels on each of them to check not only for the best possible combination of ingredients but for ones that contain the smallest number of unnecessary additives and sugars.

METHOD

1. Bring a pot of water to a boil, add the carrot and zucchini slices, and parboil them for 2 minutes. Remove the pot from the heat, pour off the hot water and run the vegetables under cold water to stop the cooking process. When cool, drain the vegetables well and set them aside.

2. In a bowl blend together the spinach, ricotta, and egg substitute and set the mix aside.

3. Cook the lasagna noodles according to the package directions.

4. Using an 8-inch by 14-inch glass baking dish, start by placing a layer of pasta along the length of the pan. Usually 2 1/2 strips will be adequate for each layer.

5. In the following order, spread some of the carrots, zucchini, spinach mix, oregano, pasta sauce and mozzarella over the noodles.

6. Repeat layering as above two more times, making sure to use the heaviest layer of mozzarella on the top.

7. Bake 45 minutes in a 375-degree oven and serve bubbling hot.

NUTRIENTS PER SERVING

CAL	PROT	CARBO	T FAT	SAT. FAT	CAL FROM FAT	CHOL	FIBER	SOD
706	49G	67G	28G	15G	35%	88MG	9G	1155MG

Sides

Sides

Ten-Minute Bean Salad

Serves 4

INGREDIENTS

1 (15-ounce) can	garbanzo beans
1 (15-ounce) can	red kidney beans
1 (15-ounce) can	black beans
1 (15-ounce) can	sweet white corn
1 medium	Vidalia or red onion–finely chopped
2 Tablespoons	olive oil
4 Tablespoons	(plus or minus) balsamic vinegar
kosher salt and freshly ground black pepper to taste	
1 Tablespoon	(plus or minus) of rosemary OR thyme OR basil OR cilantro–(choose only one.)
1 Tablespoon	fresh garlic mix (see Sweet Pepper Bouquet recipe on page 111)
½ box	fresh cherry or grape tomatoes–washed, dried and cut into halves or quarters

METHOD

1. Drain and wash all of the beans and corn.
2. Place them with the rest of the ingredients in a glass bowl, mix well, cover and chill until ready to serve.

NOTES

For variety it is possible to use fava or white cannellini beans for this dish. Another option is to add some chopped mango, clementines or mandarin oranges if a somewhat sweeter taste is desired. Refrigeration allows time for the flavors of all of the ingredients of this salad to become well integrated, but if time does not permit it may also be served at room temperature just after assembly. The beans in this recipe are an excellent source of protein and fiber.

NUTRIENTS PER SERVING

CAL	PROT	CARBO	T FAT	SAT. FAT	CAL FROM FAT	CHOL	FIBER	SOD
501	19G	83G	12G	2G	22%	0MG	16G	1320MG

White Bean, Red Onion and Radish Salad

Serves 4

INGREDIENTS

1 can	(approximately 19 ounces) white kidney beans–drained and rinsed
1/2 cup	red onion–chopped
3/4 cup	radishes–thinly sliced
1 cup	cucumber–peeled and thinly sliced or chopped
1 clove	fresh garlic–minced
1/2 cup	fresh parsley–chopped
3 Tablespoons	fresh lemon juice
2 Tablespoons	olive oil
kosher salt and freshly ground black pepper to taste	

METHOD

1. Mix all of the ingredients together in a deep bowl, cover and refrigerate several hours before serving.

NOTES

Not only is this tasty salad easy to make, it is filled with protein and fiber. And the lemon juice this salad contains is of great benefit because it slows down the digestive process and reduces the number of carbohydrates the body absorbs.

NUTRIENTS PER SERVING

CAL	PROT	CARBO	T FAT	SAT. FAT	CAL FROM FAT	CHOL	FIBER	SOD
191	8G	25G	7G	1G	34%	0MG	6G	478MG

Asian Cucumber Salad

Serves 4

INGREDIENTS

2 long	English cucumbers–washed and sliced as thinly as possible
2 teaspoons	fresh gingerroot–peeled and minced
1/4 cup	rice vinegar
1/2 teaspoon	(plus or minus) sesame oil
2 Tablespoons	sesame seeds–lightly toasted
1/4 cup	scallions–finely chopped
1/8 teaspoon	sugar (optional)

METHOD

1. Wash, dry and slice the cucumbers and place them in a bowl.
2. Grind the ginger in a food processor until it is quite fine.
3. Add the ginger and all other ingredients to the cucumbers, toss well, cover and chill in the refrigerator 1 hour or more before serving.

NOTES

Sesame seeds may be baked in a toaster oven or in the oven. Do not set the temperature above 325 degrees as the seeds burn very easily and must be carefully monitored during the baking process. Rice vinegar, sesame oil and fresh ginger are all available in most supermarkets.

NUTRIENTS PER SERVING

CAL	PROT	CARBO	T FAT	SAT. FAT	CAL FROM FAT	CHOL	FIBER	SOD
59	2G	6G	3G	1G	47%	0MG	1G	7MG

INGREDIENTS

2 teaspoons	(plus or minus) toasted sesame seeds
1/2 cup	chopped peanuts–lightly toasted
1 pound	Chinese cabbage–shredded
1/2 cup	fresh snow peas–washed and dried
1/2 cup	carrots–peeled and shredded
1/4 cup	scallions–chopped
1/2 cup	sliced pickled ginger–cut into very thin strips
1/4 cup	rice wine vinegar
2 Tablespoons	reduced-sodium soy sauce
1/4 teaspoon	(plus or minus) red pepper flakes
1 teaspoon	sesame oil

METHOD

1. Place the sesame seeds on a metal tray and bake at 325 degrees for approximately 5 minutes until they just begin to brown. When done, set them aside in a dish to cool and using the same tray repeat the roasting process with the peanuts.
2. Place the shredded cabbage in a large bowl.
3. Cut the ends off the snow peas, remove the strings that run along the length of both sides of the peas, and slice each one lengthwise into thin strips.
4. Add the snow peas, carrots, and scallions to the cabbage and mix them all together.
5. Add all the rest of the ingredients, mix well, cover and refrigerate the slaw for several hours before serving.

NOTES

Peanuts and especially sesame seeds must be watched VERY carefully during the browning process because they burn easily. All of the Asian ingredients may be purchased in both Asian markets and in many mainstream supermarkets. This recipe, whose vegetables are rich in fiber and nutrients, has the added benefit of supplying the body with the heart-healthy omega-3 trans fatty acid found in peanuts.

NUTRIENTS PER SERVING

CAL	PROT	CARBO	T FAT	SAT. FAT	CAL FROM FAT	CHOL	FIBER	SOD
123	5G	12G	7G	1G	48%	0MG	4G	677MG

Mediterranean Salad

Serves 4

INGREDIENTS

3 ripe	tomatoes—chopped
1/2	each red, yellow and green bell pepper—chopped into small pieces
2	scallions—finely chopped
1 cup	cucumber—peeled and chopped into small pieces
1/4 cup	kalamata olives—pitted and sliced
1/4 cup	feta cheese—crumbled
3 Tablespoons	(plus or minus) fresh parsley—chopped
kosher salt, freshly ground black pepper and dried oregano to taste	

METHOD

1. Mix all of the ingredients together in a bowl, cover and chill in the refrigerator until ready to serve.

NOTES

This is the type of salad that lends itself to creativity by adding 2 to 3 Tablespoons of extra-virgin olive oil, or additional seasonings such as fresh basil. It particularly complements most grilled fish preparations or gravlax served on small slices of pumpernickel bread.

NUTRIENTS PER SERVING

CAL	PROT	CARBO	T FAT	SAT. FAT	CAL FROM FAT	CHOL	FIBER	SOD
73	3G	9G	3G	2G	38%	8MG	2G	190MG

Chopped Salad with Basil and Herbes de Provence

Serves 4

INGREDIENTS

2 large	ripe tomatoes—washed and dried
1 long	English cucumber—peeled and chopped
6 to 8	radishes—finely chopped
8 to 10	(plus or minus) fresh basil leaves—shredded
1 to 2 teaspoons	(plus or minus) herbes de Provence
kosher salt and freshly ground black pepper to taste	

METHOD

1. Cut the tomatoes into small chunks and place them in a large bowl.
2. Add the rest of the ingredients to #1, mix well and serve.

NOTES

It is fun to be creative by adding as many or as few of these salad ingredients as you wish in order to adjust it to your liking. One variation, for example, would be to eliminate the herbes de Provence, add 1/4 cup (plus or minus) each of freshly chopped scallions and parsley, and top each individual portion of the salad with a dollop of fat-free sour cream. It is not necessary to add more than 1/2 teaspoon or 1 teaspoon of salt to this recipe as the dominant flavors should primarily reflect the wonderful taste of the fresh vegetables and herbs. Herbes de Provence is available in the spice section of grocery stores.

NUTRIENTS PER SERVING

CAL	PROT	CARBO	T FAT	SAT. FAT	CAL FROM FAT	CHOL	FIBER	SOD
30	1G	6G	<1G	<1G	12%	0MG	2G	12MG

Pomegranate, Goat Cheese and Walnut Salad

Serves 4

INGREDIENTS

1 head	radicchio
1 small	bunch red leaf lettuce
seeds from 1 large, ripe pomegranate	
1½ cups	walnuts–lightly toasted and chopped into medium-sized pieces
4 ounces	goat cheese–crumbled
½ cup	red wine
¼ cup	olive oil
1 Tablespoon	sugar (or sugar equivalent)
1½ Tablespoons	red-wine vinegar
kosher salt and freshly ground black pepper to taste	

METHOD

1. Place the walnuts on a metal pan and roast them over very low heat for 10 to 15 minutes until they are lightly browned. Be sure to watch them carefully as they burn easily.
2. Combine the wine and sugar in a small pot and simmer over low heat for approximately 15 minutes until the liquid is reduced by ⅓.
3. Wash and dry the lettuces, tear the leaves into medium-sized pieces and place them in a salad bowl.
4. Using a small bowl, whisk together the still-warm wine with the vinegar, oil, salt and pepper.
5. Pour the dressing over the lettuce leaves and toss well.
6. Divide the salad onto 4 individual plates and sprinkle pomegranate seeds, walnuts and goat cheese over the top of each serving.

NOTES

Besides giving this salad eye appeal with dots of glistening red color, pomegranate seeds add surprising texture as well as a delightful tangy taste. Pomegranate seeds are rather difficult to remove from their pulp. One hint to make the job easier is to cut the fruit in half across the middle and, holding each half over a bowl, sharply hit the skin around the circumference with a heavy implement, such as a hammer, and the seeds will drop into the bowl. Walnuts are a welcome addition to this salad not only because they provide great taste and texture but also because they are filled with heart-healthy omega-3 trans fatty acid.

This recipe, courtesy of **Milos** in Montreal and **Testiatoro Milos** in New York City, is made of ingredients that "evoke Christmas in the mountains of Greece."

NUTRIENTS PER SERVING

CAL	PROT	CARBO	T FAT	SAT. FAT	CAL FROM FAT	CHOL	FIBER	SOD
573	16G	21G	48G	11G	72%	30MG	4G	122MG

Photograph for this recipe appears on page 98.

Fresh Corn Salad

Serves 4

INGREDIENTS FOR SALAD

5 ears	fresh corn–cooked, cooled and sliced off the cob
1 large	red bell pepper–diced
1 medium-sized	Vidalia (or other sweet onion)–diced
1 large,	ripe tomato–diced

INGREDIENTS FOR VINAIGRETTE DRESSING

1	shallot–minced
1 teaspoon	Dijon mustard
1 clove	fresh garlic–minced
1/8 cup	balsamic vinegar
kosher salt and freshly ground black pepper to taste	
1/2 cup	extra-virgin olive oil

METHOD FOR SALAD

1. Combine all of the salad ingredients in a large bowl.

METHOD FOR VINAIGRETTE DRESSING

1. Combine the shallots, mustard, garlic, vinegar, salt and pepper in a bowl.
2. Mix the oil into #1 by pouring it in a steady stream and whisking it until the dressing is smooth.
3. Add the dressing to the vegetables, toss to coat, cover the bowl and refrigerate the salad for at least 1 hour before serving to allow the flavors to fully blend.

NOTES

It is possible to make this summer dish out of season by substituting canned or frozen corn. To preserve as much of its flavor and moisture as possible, fresh corn is best when cooked in the husk on full power in the microwave for 2 minutes per ear.

NUTRIENTS PER SERVING

CAL	PROT	CARBO	T FAT	SAT. FAT	CAL FROM FAT	CHOL	FIBER	SOD
390	5G	31G	30G	4G	65%	0MG	5G	57MG

Roasted Asparagus with Balsamic Vinegar and Sesame Seeds

Serves 4

INGREDIENTS

1 pound	medium to thick fresh asparagus
1 Tablespoon	olive oil
2 to 3 Tablespoons	balsamic vinegar
2 Tablespoons	(or more if preferred) roasted sesame seeds
kosher salt and freshly ground black pepper to taste	

NOTES

Sesame seeds burn easily, so it is important to watch them carefully during the roasting process. In another version of this dish, the sesame seeds may be replaced with a light coating of freshly ground Parmesan cheese (because Parmesan is a hard cheese it has, by comparison to most soft cheeses, a fairly low fat content).

NUTRIENTS PER SERVING

CAL	PROT	CARBO	T FAT	SAT. FAT	CAL FROM FAT	CHOL	FIBER	SOD
71	4G	7G	4G	1G	44%	0MG	2G	7MG

METHOD

1. Place the sesame seeds on a flat metal pan and roast them at 325 degrees for 2 to 3 minutes until they are lightly browned. When done, set them aside to cool.
2. Preheat the oven to 500 degrees.
3. Snap off and discard the end of each stalk of asparagus.
4. Wash the asparagus and pat them dry on paper toweling.
5. Line a flat baking pan with a sheet of aluminum foil and spread 1 tablespoon olive oil evenly over the foil.
6. Place the asparagus on the foil and roll them in the oil so that each stalk is lightly coated.
7. Arrange the asparagus so that each piece lies flat on the pan, sprinkle them with salt and pepper, place them in the oven and roast for 15 to 20 minutes. During the roasting process the pan should be gently shaken every 5 minutes to allow the asparagus to brown evenly and to avoid having them stick to the pan.
8. When done, place the asparagus on a serving dish, coat them with the balsamic vinegar, top them with the roasted sesame seeds, and serve immediately.

Sautéed Brussels Sprouts

Serves 6

INGREDIENTS

1 Tablespoon	olive oil
1 to 2 Tablespoons	fresh garlic mix (see recipe Sweet Pepper Bouquet page 111)
½ pound	fresh white pearl onions–peeled and cut in halves
1 pound	fresh Brussels sprouts–washed, dried and cut in half perpendicular to the stem so they won't fall apart when cooking
kosher salt and freshly ground black pepper to taste	

METHOD

1. Heat the olive oil in a nonstick 10-inch to 12-inch pan, add the garlic mix and onions and sauté them on medium heat until they are softened.
2. Add the Brussels sprouts, and salt and pepper to #1 and continue to sauté on medium heat until the sprouts soften but are still crunchy.
3. When done, remove the sprouts from the heat and serve at once.

NOTES

This sprout and onion combination, which is best when served hot, is a sweet and tasty way to include beneficial fiber as part of your meal.

NUTRIENTS PER SERVING

CAL	PROT	CARBO	T FAT	SAT. FAT	CAL FROM FAT	CHOL	FIBER	SOD
109	3G	11G	7G	1G	54%	0MG	4G	20MG

Sautéed Beets

Serves 6

INGREDIENTS

4 medium-sized	fresh UNPEELED red beets–washed, dried, and cut into slices ¼ inch to ½ inch thick
4 medium-sized	UNPEELED golden beets–washed, dried and cut into slices ¼ inch to ½ inch thick
1 Tablespoon	(plus or minus) fresh garlic mix (see Sweet Pepper Bouquet recipe)
kosher salt and freshly ground black pepper to taste	

NOTE

While beets contain a high amount of natural sugar, they are also rich in fiber and should be served as part of a well balanced menu that might include a portion of protein-laden grilled fish or poultry and a serving of strawberry applesauce (see recipe page 121).

METHOD

1. Place the garlic mix in a 10-inch to 12-inch nonstick skillet and cook on low to medium heat until the mix starts to soften.
2. Add the beets, salt and pepper to taste and continue cooking until the beets start to soften but are still slightly crunchy.
3. The beets may be served hot as a side dish with a high protein meal of grilled fish or chicken. Or, when cooled to room temperature, they may be served as a main dish by placing them on a bed of field greens and topping with a sprinkling of mandarin orange slices, a small amount of low-fat vinaigrette salad dressing and a dusting of crumbled blue cheese.

NUTRIENTS PER SERVING

CAL	PROT	CARBO	T FAT	SAT. FAT	CAL FROM FAT	CHOL	FIBER	SOD
68	2G	11G	2G	‹1G	30%	0MG	3G	85MG

Stir-Fry Broccoli with Shiitake Mushrooms

Serves 5

INGREDIENTS

1 Tablespoon	fresh garlic–minced
1 Tablespoon	fresh gingerroot–peeled and minced
7 Tablespoons	water (or more as needed)
1½ pounds	broccoli crowns or florets (discard the stems)–wash, dry and cut into bite-sized pieces
8 to 10	fresh shiitake mushrooms–remove and discard stems, wash and blot the caps on paper toweling, and cut each cap into ¼-inch-wide slices
4 Tablespoons	Oyster sauce
½ teaspoon	(plus or minus) sesame oil

METHOD

1. Coat a wok with a liberal amount of cooking spray and heat.
2. Add the garlic and ginger to the wok and "sweat" them over low heat until they are softened. Add 2 to 3 Tablespoons water to the mix each time it becomes too dry during the "sweating" process.
3. Add the broccoli and shiitake mushrooms and stir-fry until the mix is hot.
4. Stir the oyster sauce into the vegetables and continue to stir the mix until the vegetables are cooked crisp yet tender or to the amount desired.
5. Sprinkle with sesame oil and serve immediately.

NOTES

Because shiitake mushrooms are an excellent source of antioxidants and broccoli is high in fiber and nutritional value, this healthy, flavorful and easily prepared recipe is likely to become a heart-healthy family favorite. A broccoli floret (or crown) is the flower-like part at the top of each stem.

NUTRIENTS PER SERVING

CAL	PROT	CARBO	T FAT	SAT. FAT	CAL FROM FAT	CHOL	FIBER	SOD
57	5G	10G	1G	<1G	13%	0MG	4G	128MG

Green Beans with Dill

Serves 4

INGREDIENTS

1 pound	fresh green beans
3 to 4 Tablespoons (plus or minus) fresh dill—chopped	
juice ¼ lemon	
1 Tablespoon	nonhydrogenated butter substitute

NOTES

When preparing the dill, use only the soft fronds at the top. Discard any of the heavy parts of the stem. Not all beans have strings that run along the sides, but when present they should be removed before cooking.

METHOD

1. Wash and dry the beans. Cut off the ends, remove any strings along the sides and cut each bean in half.
2. Heat a pot of water until boiling, add the beans and cook 4 to 5 minutes until the beans are softened but still somewhat crunchy.
3. Drain the beans and place them in a serving dish.
4. Add the rest of the ingredients to #3, toss well and serve immediately.

NUTRIENTS PER SERVING

CAL	PROT	CARBO	T FAT	SAT. FAT	CAL FROM FAT	CHOL	FIBER	SOD
56	1G	7G	2G	1G	37%	0MG	4G	24MG

Zucchini and Tomato Gratin

Serves 6

INGREDIENTS

6 medium-sized	zucchini—washed and sliced
12 to 14	sliced Roma tomatoes
1 large	onion—chopped
1 teaspoon	dried oregano (or 1 Tablespoon fresh oregano)
kosher salt and freshly ground pepper to taste	
½ cup	shredded reduced-fat mozzarella cheese
2 Tablespoons	olive oil

METHOD

1. Coat a 9 x 13-inch rectangular glass or an 11-inch round ovenproof pan well with cooking spray.
2. Place the zucchini and tomato slices in the pan, making sure that they are added in alternating closely packed layers.
3. Add the onion, oregano, salt and pepper evenly over the top of the vegetables.
4. Sprinkle the cheese across the mix, drizzle olive oil over the top, bake 45 minutes in a 350-degree oven and serve immediately when done.

NOTES

It is possible to substitute for the reduced-fat mozzarella cheese with either reduced-fat asiago cheese or freshly grated Parmesan cheese. This dish is the perfect accompaniment to a dinner of well-seasoned fresh grilled fish or chicken.

NUTRIENTS PER SERVING

CAL	PROT	CARBO	T FAT	SAT. FAT	CAL FROM FAT	CHOL	FIBER	SOD
122	7G	15G	5G	1G	35%	2MG	4G	86MG

Sweet Pepper Bouquet

Serves 4

INGREDIENTS FOR PEPPERS

1 red	onion—chopped
2 yellow, 2 red and	2 orange bell peppers—washed, seeded and cut into small squares
1/4 cup	dried cranberries (and/or raisins if desired)
1/2 bunch	fresh cilantro—chopped (or chopped fresh rosemary to taste)
2 to 3 Tablespoons	balsamic vinegar (or to taste)
juice of 1/2 lime	

INGREDIENTS FOR GARLIC MIX

3 cloves	fresh garlic
2 Tablespoons	olive oil
kosher salt and fresh ground black pepper to taste	

NOTES

This versatile recipe may be used as a main dish by serving the pepper mix over a bed of such healthy and unrefined grains as whole wheat couscous or brown rice. It may also be presented as a side dish with a meal of grilled fish or chicken. Because it stores well, it is wise—especially for garlic lovers—when preparing the garlic mix to make extra to have on hand as an excellent flavoring agent to enliven, as desired, many fish and vegetable recipes of choice.

METHOD

1. Prepare the garlic mix by chopping the garlic in a food processor until the pieces are small but not puréed. Transfer the garlic to a small bowl, pour 2 Tablespoons olive oil over the top, sprinkle with a pinch of kosher salt and pepper and mash the oil, pepper, and salt into the garlic with a fork.

2. Measure 1 Tablespoon of the garlic mix into a nonstick 10-inch to 12-inch sauté pan. Add the onion and cook, stirring occasionally, on low heat until the mix starts to soften. (Extra garlic mix may be stored in a covered container in the refrigerator for up to two weeks.)

3. Add the chopped peppers, dried fruit, 1/2 of the cilantro OR rosemary, balsamic vinegar and lime juice and salt and pepper to taste and, stirring occasionally, continue to sauté until the peppers are cooked but still crunchy.

4. Add the rest of the fresh herbs according to taste, correct for seasoning as necessary and serve.

NUTRIENTS PER SERVING

CAL	PROT	CARBO	T FAT	SAT. FAT	CAL FROM FAT	CHOL	FIBER	SOD
116	2G	20G	4G	1G	28%	0MG	3G	8MG

NUTRITIONAL INFORMATION INCLUDES 1 TABLESPOON OF THE GARLIC MIX.

Elegant Eggplant

Serves 6

INGREDIENTS

¼ cup	flour (or more if needed)
kosher salt and freshly ground black pepper	
1 large	eggplant
¼ cup	egg substitute (or more if needed)
2 Tablespoons	olive oil
1 large	ripe tomato—sliced into thin rounds
1 large	sweet onion—cut into thin round slices
½ pound	crisp turkey bacon
6 slices	low-fat American cheese
fresh parsley for garnish—washed and chopped	

NOTES

Great as an informal meal, this preparation is best when accompanied by a crunchy salad of crisp romaine lightly coated with low-fat Caesar dressing.

Recipe courtesy of **Jerri Spurrier,** wife of Redskins coach Steve Spurrier

NUTRIENTS PER SERVING

CAL	PROT	CARBO	T FAT	SAT. FAT	CAL FROM FAT	CHOL	FIBER	SOD
234	14G	17G	13G	4G	49%	33MG	4G	710MG

METHOD

1. Combine the flour, salt and pepper in a flat plate.
2. Wash and slice the eggplant into ½-inch rounds.
3. Dip the eggplant rounds in the egg substitute, then coat each piece on both sides with the flour mix.
4. Heat the olive oil in a large nonstick pan and add the eggplant pieces to cook until both sides are browned.
5. Cover a large flat ovenproof pan with a layer of heavy-duty aluminum foil, coat it with a light layer of cooking spray and arrange the coated eggplant pieces in a single layer across the pan.
6. In the following order, layer each piece of eggplant with a slice of the tomato, a slice of onion, 1 to 2 slices of the crisp turkey bacon and a topping of a slice of the cheese.
7. Place the pan in the oven and broil until the cheese melts.
8. When done, remove the pan from the oven, sprinkle each of the pieces with fresh parsley and serve.

Curry-Flavored Spaghetti Squash

Serves 4

INGREDIENTS

1 medium-sized	spaghetti squash
1 Tablespoon	olive oil
1 large	onion—chopped
1/2 cup	currants
1 teaspoon	(plus or minus) curry powder
4	scallions—sliced
1/2 cup	sliced almonds—lightly toasted
1/8 teaspoon	cayenne pepper
kosher salt to taste	

NOTES

For those who like a stronger curry flavor, it is possible to add more curry powder to taste. But it's prudent to add this strongly flavored spice a little at a time. Cayenne pepper is quite hot and should be added with caution if more than just a dash is desired. The high fiber content of the squash and the antioxidants in the nuts make this an especially nutritious vegetable dish. As an alternative to baking, the squash may be cut in half and steamed until soft.

NUTRIENTS PER SERVING

CAL	PROT	CARBO	T FAT	SAT. FAT	CAL FROM FAT	CHOL	FIBER	SOD
180	5G	19G	11G	1G	51%	0MG	5G	33MG

METHOD

1. Preheat the oven to 350 degrees.
2. Cut the spaghetti squash in half and place the cut sides down on a nonstick baking pan coated lightly with cooking spray. (If a regular metal pan is used, be sure to cover it with a layer of heavy-duty aluminum foil coated with cooking spray.)
3. Place the pan in the preheated oven and bake the squash 40 minutes or until tender.
4. When done, remove #3 from the oven, and when cool, scrape the softened squash strings from the inside of each of the halves into a bowl.
5. Heat the olive oil in a large nonstick pan. Add the chopped onion and "sweat" it on low heat until it is soft but still firm.
6. Add the currants and the curry powder to #5 and continue cooking until these ingredients are well heated and combined with the onion. If the mix becomes dry, restore the moisture by adding 2 to 3 Tablespoons of water.
7. Add the cooked squash and rest of the ingredients to #6, mix well, heat through and serve.

Grilled Vegetables with Balsamic Marinade

Serves 4

INGREDIENTS FOR MARINADE

1 Tablespoon	balsamic vinegar
1 Tablespoon	tamari
1 teaspoon	salt
2 Tablespoons	olive oil
2 teaspoons	fresh garlic—minced
1/8 teaspoon	freshly ground black pepper

INGREDIENTS FOR VEGETABLES

2	carrots—peeled and cut lengthwise in halves or quarters
4	leeks (white part only)—washed and cut in half lengthwise
4 small	yellow patty pan squash—cut into halves
1 large	eggplant—cut into 8 round slices that are 1/2 inch thick
2 red	peppers—quartered and seeded
2	zucchini—quartered
8 to 12	fresh shiitake mushroom caps—stems removed and discarded
1 small	bouquet of such fresh herbs as parsley or thyme—for garnish

METHOD FOR MARINADE

1. Using a whisk, combine all of the ingredients in a small bowl.

METHOD FOR VEGETABLES

1. Preheat the broiler or grill.
2. Brush the vegetables with the marinade and spread them out on the grill or on a cookie sheet if grilling them under the broiler.
3. Grill or broil for 2 to 3 minutes on a side or until they are cooked through but still firm.
4. Divide the grilled vegetables among 4 luncheon-sized plates and garnish each with the fresh herbs before serving.

NOTES

Served as a delightful starter or as a side to a dinner of grilled fish, these colorful, nutritious and tasty vegetables offer a feast for the eyes—and for the senses.

Recipe courtesy of **Nora Poullon,**
Restaurant Nora, Asia Nora

NUTRIENTS PER SERVING

CAL	PROT	CARBO	T FAT	SAT. FAT	CAL FROM FAT	CHOL	FIBER	SOD
242	8G	41G	8G	1G	27%	0MG	12G	871MG

Savory French Green Lentils

Serves 6

INGREDIENTS

1 Tablespoon	extra-virgin olive oil
1 Tablespoon	nonhydrogenated butter substitute
2	leeks–wash well, dry and chop the white and tender green parts
2	carrots–peeled and diced
2 ribs	celery–diced
2 cloves	garlic–minced
2	bay leaves
1 cup	dry white wine
2 cups	French green lentils
3 to 4 cups	nonfat chicken broth
1 cup	fresh mint–coarsely chopped
kosher or sea salt and fresh ground black pepper to taste	

METHOD

1. Place the olive oil and butter substitute in a 4-quart pot and heat.
2. When melted, stir in the leeks, carrots, celery, garlic and bay leaves, cover the pot and simmer on low to medium heat for 7 to 10 minutes until the vegetables are softened.
3. Add the white wine and simmer 2 to 3 minutes.
4. Add the lentils and broth and, with the pot partially covered, cook for 30 to 40 minutes until the lentils are tender.
5. Remove the pot from the heat and add the chopped mint and salt and pepper to taste.
6. Remove the bay leaves and serve.

NOTES

Lentils, a wonderful source of protein and fiber, are high in carbohydrates. Grilled or baked fish and a fresh salad of choice are suggested accompaniments for a well-balanced meal.

NUTRIENTS PER SERVING

CAL	PROT	CARBO	T FAT	SAT. FAT	CAL FROM FAT	CHOL	FIBER	SOD
303	18G	44G	4G	1G	12%	0MG	11G	475MG

Saffron-Flavored Basmati Rice

Serves 4

INGREDIENTS

1 cup	basmati rice
1 to 2 Tablespoons	nonhydrogenated butter substitute
1 medium-sized	shallot—finely chopped
1½ cups	water or nonfat chicken broth
kosher salt to taste	
¼ teaspoon	saffron threads—crumbled

NOTES

This saffron flavored variation of the recipe for perfect basmati rice is a wonderful foil for such preparations as Spanish-Style Shrimp (see recipe page 93), Moroccan Lemon Chicken (see recipe page 70) and most varieties of grilled or broiled fish.

NUTRIENTS PER SERVING

CAL	PROT	CARBO	T FAT	SAT. FAT	CAL FROM FAT	CHOL	FIBER	SOD
223	3G	46G	5G	1G	17%	0MG	1G	45MG

METHOD

1. Place the rice in a sieve, wash it under cold running water until the water runs clear, and drain well.
2. Melt the butter substitute in a 2-quart pot, add the shallots and "sweat" them on low heat until they soften.
3. Add the rice and the water, cover the pot and bring the liquid to a boil.
4. Stir the salt and crumbled saffron into the rice, replace the cover and lower the heat so that the rice simmers for approximately 10 minutes or until all of the water has been absorbed.
5. Turn off the heat, stir the rice once again, replace the cover and let the rice rest for at least 10 minutes before serving.

Perfect Basmati Rice

Serves 4

INGREDIENTS

1 cup	basmati rice
1¼ cups	cold water
1 teaspoon	(plus or minus) kosher salt

NOTES

Even though basmati rice is a starch, it differs from others in its molecular composition, which makes it more resistant to quick digestion and insulin spikes. Basmati, with its rich and uniquely aromatic nutty flavor is widely available in mainstream grocery and specialty markets.

NUTRIENTS PER SERVING

CAL	PROT	CARBO	T FAT	SAT. FAT	CAL FROM FAT	CHOL	FIBER	SOD
180	3G	45G	0G	0G	0%	0MG	1G	470MG

METHOD

1. Place the rice in a sieve and wash it under cold running water until the water runs clear.
2. Add the rice, water and salt to a 2-quart pot, cover it and bring the water to a boil.
3. Turn down the heat, stir the mix, replace the cover and simmer 10 minutes or until all the water is absorbed.
4. Remove the pot from the heat, stir the rice, and let it sit covered for at least 10 minutes more before serving.

Wild Rice with Cranberries

Serves 6

INGREDIENTS

2	shallots–finely chopped
2 cloves	garlic–finely chopped
2½ cups	water
1 cup	wild rice
1 Tablespoon	kosher salt (or to taste)
freshly ground pepper to taste	
1 to 2 teaspoons	dried thyme
2	bay leaves
½ teaspoon	dried savory
rind of 1 lemon–finely chopped	
1 ounce	dried cranberries
1 to 2 ounces	toasted pecans–chopped

METHOD

1. Coat the bottom of a 1-quart pot with cooking spray, add the shallots and garlic and "sweat" them on low heat until the vegetables soften.
2. Add the water to #1, bring it to a boil and mix in the rice, salt, pepper, thyme, bay leaves, savory, lemon rind and cranberries.
3. Cover the pot, reduce the heat to low and cook the rice 45 minutes to 1 hour until the water is absorbed and the rice is soft.
5. Scatter the pecans over the top of the rice when ready to serve.

NOTES

Wild rice is a natural long grain rice that has a dense and distinctive nutty flavor. It is possible to prepare this recipe in advance and heat it in the oven or microwave before serving. In addition to serving the rice as an elegant accompaniment to fish or chicken preparations, this recipe may be used as a stuffing for Cornish game hens (see recipe page 74). If possible, remove and discard the bay leaves before serving.

NUTRIENTS PER SERVING

CAL	PROT	CARBO	T FAT	SAT. FAT	CAL FROM FAT	CHOL	FIBER	SOD
198	5G	29G	7G	1G	32%	0MG	3G	942MG

Sweets

Sweets

Strawberry Applesauce

INGREDIENTS

1 (46- to 48-ounce) jar natural unsweetened applesauce	
1 (16-ounce) bag	unsweetened frozen strawberries
3 Tablespoons	sugar or sugar equivalent (or more to taste)

NOTES

Strawberry applesauce is a particular favorite with children. Almost dessert-like in taste, it provides them with nutritional benefits they can really enjoy!

METHOD

1. Defrost the strawberries.
2. Empty the entire jar of applesauce into a deep mixing bowl.
3. Purée the defrosted strawberries in a food processor.
4. Add the strawberries and the sugar (or sugar equivalent) to #2, mix well and refrigerate before serving.

NUTRIENTS PER SERVING

CAL	PROT	CARBO	T FAT	SAT. FAT	CAL FROM FAT	CHOL	FIBER	SOD
111	1G	29G	<1G	<1G	1%	0MG	3G	5MG

Baked Apples

Serves 6

INGREDIENTS

2 Tablespoons	currants
1/2 cup	walnuts–chopped
1/4 teaspoon	ground cinnamon
1/8 teaspoon	grated nutmeg
6	Granny Smith apples
1/2 cup	orange juice
1/4 cup	dried apricots–finely chopped
1/2 cup	honey
3 Tablespoons	nonhydrogenated butter substitute
1 1/4 cups	apple cider

NOTES

Baked apples are best when served hot or warm. If the apples are prepared ahead, they may be heated in the oven before serving. However, care must be taken not to let the apples become overcooked to the point where the skins split, allowing the apples to fall apart. As a special treat, each apple may be served with a topping of a small scoop of nonfat vanilla yogurt.

NUTRIENTS PER SERVING

CAL	PROT	CARBO	T FAT	SAT. FAT	CAL FROM FAT	CHOL	FIBER	SOD
295	2G	54G	10G	2G	28%	0MG	4G	53MG

METHOD

1. Preheat the oven to 375 degrees.
2. Mix the currants, walnuts, cinnamon and nutmeg together and set aside.
3. With a vegetable peeler, remove the skin from the top 1/3 of each apple.
4. Remove the seeds and pith from the inside of each apple with an apple corer, taking care not to pierce the bottom of the apple in the process.
5. Prick the peeled flesh of each apple several times with a fork.
6. Closely arrange the apples side by side in an ovenproof glass baking dish.
7. Sprinkle the cavity and the peeled portion of each apple with the orange juice. Add an equal portion of the apricots to each cavity.
8. Fill the cavity of each of the apples with an equal portion of the currant/walnut mix.
9. Pour the honey over each apple and dot each one with a topping of nonhydrogenated butter substitute.
10. Pour the cider over the apples and let it pool around the bottom of the baking plate.
11. Place the uncovered apples in the oven and bake them for 40 to 50 minutes, basting them often with the cooking liquid.
12. The apples are done when they just begin to soften. At that point, remove them from the oven and set them aside until ready to serve.

Apple Tart

Serves 8

INGREDIENTS FOR TART

1	ready-made pastry crust
5 large	Granny Smith apples—peeled, seeded and evenly cut into approximately ¹/₈-inch slices
4 Tablespoons	nonhydrogenated butter substitute
¹/₂ cup	sugar

INGREDIENTS FOR GLAZE

4 Tablespoons	reduced-sugar or sugarless apricot preserves
2 teaspoons	water
1 teaspoon	sugar (or sugar substitute)

NOTES

While the tart crust is, unfortunately, made with saturated fat, only a modest amount of it is present per serving. The rest of the ingredients are entirely fat-free. The crust has a better chance of browning if it is brushed on the inside with a fine layer of raw egg white before the apples are added. In place of ¹/₂ cup of sugar to coat the apples, try using ¹/₄ cup sugar mixed with the same amount of sugar substitute (see source product list page 136).

NUTRIENTS PER SERVING

CAL	PROT	CARBO	T FAT	SAT. FAT	CAL FROM FAT	CHOL	FIBER	SOD
286	1G	44G	12G	1G	38%	8MG	2G	188MG

METHOD

1. Preheat the oven to 400 degrees.
2. Roll out the crust and place it in a tart pan.
3. Arrange the apple slices on the crust in close overlapping circles.
4. Dot the top of the apples with the small pieces of the butter substitute and sprinkle ¹/₂ cup sugar evenly over the top.
5. Place the tart in the oven and bake it for 15 minutes.
6. Then, turn the heat down to 375 degrees and continue baking another 25 minutes.
7. When done, remove the tart from the oven and set it aside.
8. To make the glaze for the top of the tart, place the apricot preserves, water and sugar (or sugar equivalent) in a small pot. Heat the mix on a stove burner until it is hot and melted. Use a spoon to mash the preserves into the other ingredients while heating.
9. While the tart is still warm, spread the entire top of the tart with a thin layer of the glaze.
10. If possible, serve the tart while it is warm. Top each small wedge-shaped serving with a scoop of nonfat frozen vanilla yogurt or with a small amount of non-dairy whipped topping.

Dried Fruit Tart

Serves 10

INGREDIENTS

2 cups	pitted prunes
2 cups	dried apricots
1 cup	dried unsweetened sour cherries
1/2 cup	dried unsweetened apple slices
small slivers of the skin of 1/2 lemon	
1 1/2 cups	apple cider
1	ready-made refrigerated pie crust
1	raw egg white—slightly beaten
1 cup	chopped walnuts—lightly toasted
3/4 cup	sugar—or use part sugar and part sugar substitute (see product source page 136)
4 Tablespoons	nonhydrogenated butter substitute (divided into small bits)

NOTES

It is best to cut small slices of this tart when serving because, although it is high in fiber, it is also quite rich in content and high in carbohydrates. For an extra treat, each slice may be served with a scoop of nonfat vanilla frozen yogurt or with a squirt of nonfat whipped dairy topping.

METHOD

1. Place all of the fruit, lemon skin and the cider in a covered saucepan and heat the mix until it simmers. Stirring occasionally, continue to cook for about 10 minutes or until all of the cider has been absorbed by the fruit. When done, set the pan aside to cool.
2. Preheat the oven to 375 degrees.
3. Roll out the pastry dough and place it in an 11-inch tart pan.
4. Brush the entire face-up surface of the dough with a small amount of raw egg white. This will allow the crust to brown well during the baking process and act as a barrier to prevent any liquid from the fruit from seeping through the crust while cooking.
5. Chop the fruit coarsely, place it in a bowl and mix in the nuts, sugar and butter substitute.
6. Spread #5 evenly over the surface of the dough and bake the tart in the oven for 40 minutes.

NUTRIENTS PER SERVING

CAL	PROT	CARBO	T FAT	SAT. FAT	CAL FROM FAT	CHOL	FIBER	SOD
489	5G	85G	18G	2G	31%	6MG	6G	164MG

Peach Melba

Serves 4

INGREDIENTS

12 ounces	nonfat frozen vanilla yogurt
2 medium to large ripe peaches–peeled and sliced	
2 Tablespoons	fresh raspberry sauce (see recipe page 130)
6	plain, thin chocolate cookie wafers
1 pint	fresh raspberries–washed and well drained
non-dairy whipped cream–optional	

NOTES

A wonderful blend of taste and color, this easy-to-make dessert is always a showstopper! If desired, each dish may be crowned with a squirt of non-dairy whipped topping.

NUTRIENTS PER SERVING

CAL	PROT	CARBO	T FAT	SAT. FAT	CAL FROM FAT	CHOL	FIBER	SOD
254	5G	54G	2G	<1G	6%	1MG	7G	155MG

Photograph for this recipe appears on page 118.

METHOD

1. Place a 3-ounce scoop of the nonfat vanilla yogurt in the center of each of 4 individual dessert-sized bowls and arrange the slices from 1/2 peach around the yogurt.
2. Spoon 1 to 2 Tablespoons of the raspberry sauce over each portion.
3. Arrange 2 chocolate wafers on the sides of each dish, scatter fresh raspberries over each portion and serve immediately.

Oven-Poached Pears with Blueberries

Serves 4

INGREDIENTS

4	Bosc pears–peeled and cored
½ cup	Gewürztraminer wine
1 Tablespoon	sugar
1 Tablespoon	orange zest
2	vanilla beans–split
¼ cup	fresh blueberries

NOTES

If desired, additional fresh orange zest may be scattered over the top of each pear when serving. This versatile and 121-calorie-per-serving dessert may also be made by substituting red wine for the Gewürztraminer and dried currants for the blueberries. Another version would be the replacement of the Gewürztraminer and blueberries with Champagne and fresh red currants.

Recipe courtesy of **Bill Holman**, *Design Cuisine*

METHOD

1. After peeling and coring the pears, place them in a baking dish.
2. Pour the wine over the fruit.
3. Sprinkle the pears with the sugar and orange zest and top each with a section of vanilla bean.
4. Cover tightly with foil and bake the pears in a 300-degree oven for 30 to 45 minutes or until the fruit is tender.
5. Discard the vanilla beans after the pears are cooked.
6. To serve, spoon 1 pear and some of the syrup into a small dessert dish and sprinkle each portion with blueberries.

NUTRIENTS PER SERVING

CAL	PROT	CARBO	T FAT	SAT. FAT	CAL FROM FAT	CHOL	FIBER	SOD
121	1G	26G	1G	‹1G	4%	0MG	4G	2MG

Lemon Bread

Each loaf serves 8

INGREDIENTS FOR BREAD

1/2 cup	unsalted butter
1/2 cup	nonhydrogenated butter substitute
1 3/4 cups	sugar
2	eggs
1/2 cup	liquid egg substitute
2 teaspoons	baking powder
2 1/2 cups	flour
1 cup	skim milk
3/4 cup	walnuts–chopped
grated peel of 2 lemons	

INGREDIENTS FOR BREAD TOPPING

1/3 cup	sugar
juice of 2 lemons	

NOTES

This recipe, which makes 2 loaves, may be served upon cooling or may be either stored in the refrigerator for several days or in the freezer for several months when wrapped well in foil and placed in a tightly sealed plastic bag. Originally these breads contained twice the amount of butter and eggs, and whole milk rather than skim. Lemon bread is the perfect foil at any time of the year when served with a topping of sliced fresh seasonal fruits or berries accompanied by a small scoop of fat-free yogurt or a Tablespoon or two of fresh raspberry sauce (see recipe page 130).

METHOD

1. Preheat the oven to 350 degrees.
2. In a large, deep bowl cream together the butter and butter substitute with 1 3/4 cups sugar.
3. In a small bowl beat the eggs and liquid egg substitute together, mix in the baking powder and, when fully combined, add it to #2.
4. Stir the flour and the milk in alternating amounts into #3 until the ingredients are well blended.
5. Add the nuts and lemon rind to #4 and mix well.
6. Generously coat 2 ovenproof glass loaf pans with cooking spray.
7. Divide the batter equally between the 2 pans and bake at 350 degrees for 50 to 60 minutes or until a cake tester comes out clean when inserted into the center of each loaf.
8. While the breads are cooking, combine 1/3 cup sugar with the juice of 2 lemons.
9. As soon as the breads are removed from the oven, pierce the entire top of the loaves with a toothpick and pour the lemon/sugar mixture evenly over each.
10. Allow the breads to cool completely on wire racks before removing them from the pans.

NUTRIENTS PER SERVING

CAL	PROT	CARBO	T FAT	SAT. FAT	CAL FROM FAT	CHOL	FIBER	SOD
626	10G	87G	28G	11G	40%	84MG	2G	278MG

Pumpkin Bread

Serves 8

INGREDIENTS

1³/₄ cups	flour
1 teaspoon	salt
1 Tablespoon	baking soda
¹/₂ teaspoon	nutmeg (plus or minus)
¹/₂ teaspoon	cinnamon (plus or minus)
¹/₂ teaspoon	ground cloves
¹/₂ cup	vegetable oil
1¹/₂ cups	sugar
1	egg
¹/₄ cup	liquid egg substitute
1¹/₄ cups	canned pumpkin
grated peel from ¹/₂ fresh lemon	
¹/₂ cup	chopped walnuts
¹/₂ small box	of raisins (optional)

NOTES

It is important that a cake tester be used to determine if the bread is cooked through at the end of the baking period. The tester should come out clean after inserting it into the middle of the loaf. If there is any liquid residue on it, the bread should be allowed to bake approximately 3 to 5 more minutes. This recipe was originally made with 2 whole eggs. It might be possible to substitute for half of the sugar by replacing it with a sugar equivalent (see product source list). Pumpkin Bread can be enjoyed plain or topped for dessert with a scoop of nonfat frozen vanilla yogurt.

METHOD

1. Preheat the oven to 350 degrees.
2. Combine the flour, salt, baking soda, nutmeg, cinnamon and cloves, sift them into a bowl and set the mix aside.
3. Prepare a nonstick loaf pan by coating it with cooking spray. Set it aside until it is ready to be used.
4. Place the oil and sugar in a deep bowl and, using an electric mixer, blend them together.
5. Beat in the egg and then add the egg substitute.
6. Next beat in the pumpkin and the lemon peel followed by the nuts, raisins and flour mixture. Combine all of the ingredients for the batter so that they are well integrated.
7. Fill the loaf pan with the batter (it should be no more than ³/₄ full), place it in the preheated oven and bake it for 1 hour and 10 minutes.

NUTRIENTS PER SERVING

CAL	PROT	CARBO	T FAT	SAT. FAT	CAL FROM FAT	CHOL	FIBER	SOD
440	6G	62G	20G	2G	39%	27MG	3G	789MG

Baked French Toast with Berries

Serves 8

INGREDIENTS

1/4 cup	nonhydrogenated butter substitute
1 (8- to 9-ounce) loaf day old sourdough bread	
3/4 cup	liquid egg substitute
3 Tablespoons	sugar
1 teaspoon	vanilla extract
2 1/4 cups	skim milk
1/2 cup	all-purpose flour
6 Tablespoons	dark brown sugar, packed
1/2 teaspoon	ground cinnamon
1 cup	fresh or frozen blueberries
1 cup	fresh or frozen strawberries

NOTES

Much of the fat and some of the high glycemic carbohydrate content of the original recipe was reduced by using sourdough instead of French bread, replacing eggs with egg substitute, using skim in place of whole milk, and substituting nonhydrogenated butter substitute for butter. This preparation is a natural when served for brunch and a surprise when served warm as a dessert item topped with a small scoop of nonfat vanilla frozen yogurt.

NUTRIENTS PER SERVING

CAL	PROT	CARBO	T FAT	SAT. FAT	CAL FROM FAT	CHOL	FIBER	SOD
271	9G	46G	6G	2G	19%	1MG	2G	344MG

METHOD

1. Grease the inside of a 9 x 13-inch ovenproof glass baking dish well with 1 Tablespoon of the butter substitute.
2. Cut the bread on the diagonal into 1-inch slices and place them in the baking dish.
3. In a medium-sized bowl lightly beat the egg substitute, sugar and vanilla. Then whisk in the milk until the ingredients are well blended.
4. Pour #3 over the bread, turning the pieces to coat them well with the liquid.
5. Cover and refrigerate the dish overnight.
6. When ready to cook, preheat the oven to 375 degrees.
7. Combine the flour, brown sugar and cinnamon in a small bowl. Using a cutting motion with 2 regular tableware knives, cut small pieces of the butter substitute into the flour, brown sugar and cinnamon until the mixture resembles coarse crumbs.
8. Turn over the bread in the baking dish, scatter it with the blueberries and sprinkle the top evenly with the crumb mixture.
9. Place the uncovered dish in the oven and bake 40 minutes or until golden brown.
10. Cut the toast into squares and top each piece with strawberries when serving.

Fresh Raspberry Sauce

Serves 6

INGREDIENTS

1 (16-ounce) bag	frozen unsweetened raspberries
1 Tablespoon	(or more) sugar or sugar equivalent
1 teaspoon	raspberry liqueur

NOTES

Refreshing and versatile, this sauce brings the taste of summer with it—all year round! The rich taste belies the fact that it is not rich in content. The intense flavor of this sauce enhances not only the Peach Melba recipe it was designed for (see recipe page 125) but is perfect when spooned over Lemon Bread (see recipe page 127), or a bowl of fresh, ripe seasonal berries.

NUTRIENTS PER SERVING

CAL	PROT	CARBO	T FAT	SAT. FAT	CAL FROM FAT	CHOL	FIBER	SOD
86	1G	22G	<1G	0G	1%	0MG	3G	1MG

METHOD

1. Defrost the raspberries and place them in a 2-quart saucepan.
2. Bring the berries to a boil and cook for 1 to 2 minutes.
3. Pour the berries into a strainer placed over a heatproof bowl and, with the back of a spoon, mash them through the strainer to extract as much of the juice and pulp as possible.
4. Discard the seeds, return the liquid to the pot, add the sugar and heat until the mixture boils for another minute.
5. Remove the raspberry syrup from the flame and when cool, mix in the liqueur.
6. Transfer the sauce to a bowl, cover, and store it in the refrigerator until ready for use.

Nut Balls

Serves 8 (based on 2 nut balls per person)

INGREDIENTS

1/4 pound	nonhydrogenated butter substitute
1 cup	flour
1 cup	walnuts—finely chopped
2 teaspoons	vanilla extract
1 teaspoon	water
4 Tablespoons	powdered sugar
1/4 cup	powdered sugar

NOTES

The replacement of saturated fat with the nonhydrogenated butter substitute is ideal for this recipe, and the walnuts provide a good source of omega-3 trans fatty acid.

NUTRIENTS PER SERVING

CAL	PROT	CARBO	T FAT	SAT. FAT	CAL FROM FAT	CHOL	FIBER	SOD
249	4G	21G	17G	3G	61%	0MG	1G	92MG

METHOD

1. Preheat the oven to 325 degrees.
2. Place the butter substitute in a deep bowl and let it warm to room temperature.
3. Add the flour, walnuts, vanilla extract, water and 4 Tablespoons of powdered sugar to #2 and, using your hand, blend them completely together.
4. Roll small portions of the dough into 16 uniform balls, place them on a metal baking sheet and bake them in the oven for 20 to 25 minutes.
5. While the cookies are baking, place 1/4 cup powdered sugar in a bowl and set it aside.
6. When the cookies are done, remove the pan from the oven and, while the balls are still hot, roll each one in the sugar.
7. Place them on a platter to cool completely before serving.

No-Bake Blueberry Pie

Serves 8

INGREDIENTS

1	ready-made pie crust
3 pints	blueberries
1/2 cup	water
1 cup	sugar
juice of 1/2 lemon	
4 heaping Tablespoons cornstarch	

NOTES

For an added treat when serving, top each slice of pie with a small scoop of nonfat vanilla yogurt.

NUTRIENTS PER SERVING

CAL	PROT	CARBO	T FAT	SAT. FAT	CAL FROM FAT	CHOL	FIBER	SOD
294	1G	56G	8G	‹1G	24%	8MG	3G	147MG

METHOD

1. Preheat the oven to 450 degrees.
2. Roll out the pie dough to fit a 9-inch deep-dish pie plate.
3. Line the pie plate with the dough, prick it well over the entire crust with a fork and bake it in the oven 5 to 7 minutes until lightly browned. During the baking process BE SURE to check the crust often and prick it again with a fork if the dough starts to rise up out of the pie plate.
4. When done, remove the crust from the oven and set it aside to cool.
5. Place one pint of cleaned berries, along with the water, sugar and lemon juice, in a deep 2-quart pot. Bring the mixture to a boil and cook it until the skins of all of the berries burst open.
6. Arrange a handheld strainer over a bowl, pour the hot berry mix into the strainer and mash the berries against the side of the strainer with the back of a large spoon in order to extract all the juice.
7. Discard the skins and return the blueberry liquid to the pot.
8. Place 4 Tablespoons of cornstarch in a small custard cup and add just enough cold water to completely dissolve the cornstarch.
9. Bring the blueberry liquid to a rapid boil and, stirring constantly, add the cornstarch to the boiling liquid in a slow and steady stream until the mixture becomes quite thick and sludgy.
10. Immediately remove the pot from the heat and quickly mix the remaining 2 pints of cleaned berries into the hot berry syrup.
11. Pour the mix into the pie shell and refrigerate several hours until firm.

Key Lime Pie

Serves 8

INGREDIENTS FOR CRUST

1 (9-ounce) box	plain thin chocolate cookie wafers (see recommended products list)
3 Tablespoons	nonhydrogenated butter substitute
4 Tablespoons	unsalted butter

INGREDIENTS FOR PIE FILLING

grated rind of one of the limes

1/2 cup	fresh lime juice (approximately 3 to 4 limes)
4	egg whites—stiffly beaten (do not use packaged egg whites)
1 1/2 packages	plain gelatin
2	egg yolks
1 (14-ounce) can	nonfat sweetened condensed milk

METHOD FOR CRUST

1. Preheat oven to 350 degrees.
2. Place the cookies in a food processor, grind them into fine particles and pour them into a large bowl.
3. Melt the butter substitute and butter together, pour the hot liquid into the crumbs and blend the mix with a fork until the ingredients are well combined.
4. Lightly coat a 9-inch deep-dish pie plate with cooking spray.
5. Using a fork, spread the cookie mix evenly over the surface of the pie plate, place the plate in the oven, bake for 8 minutes and set aside to cool.

METHOD FOR PIE ASSEMBLY

1. Wash and dry the limes.
2. Grate the skin of one of the limes into a small bowl.
3. Add the lime juice to the same bowl and set it aside.
4. Crack open 4 eggs, place the whites only in a medium-sized bowl and whip them until they are quite stiff.
5. Mix the gelatin into the lime juice so that it dissolves for a few minutes before use.
6. Discard two of the yolks, place the remaining two yolks in a large bowl and beat lightly.
7. Add the condensed milk and lime juice and beat until all of the ingredients are combined.
8. Fold egg whites into #7.
9. Pour the mix into the chocolate pie shell and refrigerate several hours before serving.

NOTES

If desired when serving, top each piece of pie with a small amount of non-dairy whipped cream. Not only was this dessert formerly made with 8 Tablespoons butter, 4 egg yolks and a can of regular sweetened condensed milk, it was also topped with 1/2 pint of whipped heavy cream. For those who object to using raw egg yolks in a recipe, this pie may be made without the yolks but with the addition of an extra half-packet of unflavored gelatin added to the lime juice as above. The elimination of the yolks and addition of the gelatin changes the texture of the pie to a looser, more chiffon-like consistency. When making the recipe without the yolks, it is also possible to eliminate the crust and simply pour the filling into individual custard cups, refrigerate them for several hours and serve them accompanied by 2 thin chocolate cookie wafers per person.

NUTRIENTS PER SERVING

CAL	PROT	CARBO	T FAT	SAT. FAT	CAL FROM FAT	CHOL	FIBER	SOD
411	10G	53G	19G	9G	40%	88MG	1G	359MG

Acknowledgments

Our deepest appreciation to those who helped bring this project to reality:

Recipe Contributors: Jane Abrams, Katherine Andringa, Patty Perkins Andringa, Bryna Bell, Arlene Cherner, Laurie Coughlin, Andrea Fraser-Reid Farr, Nancy Korman, Mildred Lurie, Toni McHugh, Janna Oxman, Patti Sowalsky, Richard Sowalsky, Susan Sowalsky, BJ Strodel, and George Theodoris.

Marketing Committee: Bonnie Baum, Jane-Scott Cantus, Nancy Chistolini, Laurie Coughlin, Sandy Haller, Charlotte Cameron Marshall, Ellen Moore, Janna Oxman, Julie Rosenthal, Nina Santos, Nina Sirianni, and Carmencita Whonder.

Special Friends: Creative Associates International, Inc., Patti Cumming, Sally Chapoton, Heather Freeman, Diana Goldberg, Colleen Herlihy, Lisa Mezzetti, Michelle Pablo, Deborah Pine, Janet Staihar, Meg Robinson, Jerry Sowalsky, and Darlene Taylor.

Consulting Physicians: Dr. Michael Rabbino and Dr. Joseph D. Robinson.

Boys & Girls Clubs of Greater Washington Staff: Patricia G. Shannon, President; Nikole Brown, Director of Marketing; and Sharon Ruiz, Director of Special Events.

Photographer: Ed Whitman, Lightstruck Studio
Food Stylist: Robin Lutz

Participating Restaurants, Caterers and Celebrity Chefs:
Amonwadee "Dee" Buizer, Chef, Sweet Basil Gourmet Thai Cuisine
Susan Gage, Susan Gage Caterers
Darrell Green, former Redskins cornerback and founder of the Darrell Green Youth Life Foundation (DGYLF)
William Holman, Partner, Design Cuisine
Michael Kaiser, President, The John F. Kennedy Center for the Performing Arts
Rob Klink, Executive Chef, The Oceanaire Seafood Room
Milos of Milos Montreal & Estiatoro Milos, NYC
Morou, Executive Chef, Signatures
Franco Nuschese, Host, Café Milano
Nora Poullon, Restaurant Nora & Asia Nora
Michel Richard, Executive Chef and Owner, Citronelle
Leonard Slatkin, Music Director, National Symphony Orchestra
Jerri Spurrier, wife of Washington Redskins Head Coach, Steve Spurrier

Nutritional Profile Guidelines

The editors have attempted to present these family recipes in a format that allows approximate nutritional values to be computed. Persons with dietary or health problems or whose diets require close monitoring should not rely solely on the nutritional information provided. They should consult their physician or a registered dietitian for specific information.

Abbreviations for Nutritional Profile

Cal — Calories	T Fat — Total Fat	Sod — Sodium
Prot — Protein	Chol — Cholesterol	g — grams
Carbo — Carbohydrates	Fiber — Dietary Fiber	mg — milligrams

Nutritional information for these recipes is computed from information derived from many sources, including materials supplied by the United States Department of Agriculture, computer databanks, and journals in which the information is assumed to be in the public domain. However, many specialty items, new products, and processed foods may not be available from these sources or may vary from the average values used in these profiles. More information on new and/or specific products may be obtained by reading the nutrient labels. Unless otherwise specified, the nutritional profile of these recipes is based on all measurements being level.

- Artificial sweeteners vary in use and strength and should be used to taste, using the recipe ingredients as a guideline. Sweeteners using aspartame (NutraSweet® and Equal®) should not be used as a sweetener in recipes involving prolonged heating, which reduces the sweet taste. For further information on the use of these sweeteners, refer to the package.
- Alcoholic ingredients have been analyzed for the basic information. Cooking causes the evaporation of alcohol, which decreases alcoholic and caloric content.
- Buttermilk, sour cream, and yogurt are the types available commercially.
- Canned beans and vegetables have been analyzed with the canning liquid. Rinsing and draining canned products will lower the sodium content.
- Chicken, cooked for boning and chopping, has been roasted; this method yields the lowest caloric values.
- Eggs are all large. To avoid raw eggs that may carry salmonella, as in eggnog or 6-week muffin batter, use an equivalent amount of commercial egg substitute.
- Flour is unsifted all-purpose flour.
- Garnishes, serving suggestions, and other optional information are not included in the profile.
- Margarine and butter are regular, not whipped or presoftened.
- Oil is any type of vegetable cooking·oil. Shortening is hydrogenated vegetable shortening.
- Ingredients to taste have not been included in the nutritional profile.
- If a choice of ingredients has been given, the profile reflects the first option. If a choice of amounts has been given, the profile reflects the greater amount.

Source List for Editor's Recommended Products

Smart Balance®.....nonhydrogenated butter substitute

Egg Beaters®......liquid egg substitute

Splenda®......sugar equivalent

Smart Beat®......fat-free mayonnaise

Kraft® Free Mayonnaise Dressing......fat-free mayonnaise

Lee Kum Kee®......black bean sauce with garlic

Nabisco® Famous Chocolate Wafers

Classico® Pasta Sauce

Bibliography

Fat Land by Greg Critser

Fast Food Facts by Marion J. Franz, MS, RD, LD, CDE

Calories and Carbohydrates by Barbara Kraus

Calories, Carbs and Sugar by Linda McDonald, MS, RD

The Fat Counter by Annette B. Natow, PhD, RD, and Jo-Ann Heslin, MA, RD

The Corrine T. Netzer Encyclopedia of Food Values

The Doctor's Pocket Calorie, Fat & Carbohydrate Counter by Allan Rorushek, Nutritionist

Complete Guide to Carb Counting by Hope S. Warshaw, MMSc, RD, CDE, and Karmeen Kulkarni, MS, RD, CDE

The Good Carb Cookbook by Sandra Woodruff, MS, RD

Consulting Physicians

Michael Rabbino, MD

Joseph D. Robinson, MD

Glossary

Baste: Moistening ingredients periodically during the cooking process by using the pan juices or other prescribed liquid.

Caramelize: To sauté until the ingredients appear glazed or lightly browned.

Cream: The process of combining wet and dry ingredients together until they are completely integrated.

Cut in: Mixing fat into flour by drawing two flat kitchen knives or a pastry cutter through the ingredients until the desired consistency is reached.

Dice: To cut ingredients into very small uniform pieces.

Florets: Also known as crowns, florets are the flower-like clusters at the top of broccoli or cauliflower.

Grease: Using a very small amount of fat or cooking oil to evenly coat a utensil to prepare it for cooking.

Mince: To cut ingredients into the smallest pieces possible.

Purée: Blending or processing raw or cooked foods until they form a smooth, homogenized mix.

Sauté: To soften food by cooking it in a small amount of fat or oil.

Shred: To cut or tear food lengthwise into thin strips.

Simmer: Reducing the heat of boiling liquid to the point where the liquid remains hot but shows slight movement on the surface.

Sweat: The process of softening raw food on a low heat setting in a cooking utensil coated with a bare amount of fat or oil and adding two to three tablespoons of water each time the mix begins to dry out.

Index

Index

Index

Index

Order Information

Name: _____

Address (no PO boxes): _____

City: _____ State: _____ Zip: _____

Daytime phone with area code: _____ Email: _____

YOUR ORDER	QTY	TOTAL
Price per book: $19.95		
Shipping & handling: $3.50 per book		
Sales Tax (for MD residents only): $ .85 per book		
TOTAL:		

PAYMENT

☐ Check enclosed, made payable to BGCGW

☐ Visa   ☐ MasterCard   ☐ American Express

Card # _____

Expiration Date _____

Name as listed on card _____

Signature _____

SEND TO

Cookbook
Boys & Girls Clubs of Greater Washington
8555 16th Street, Suite 400
Silver Spring, MD 20910

For questions or quantity orders,
please call 301.562.2001.

- -

Name: _____

Address (no PO boxes): _____

City: _____ State: _____ Zip: _____

Daytime phone with area code: _____ Email: _____

YOUR ORDER	QTY	TOTAL
Price per book: $19.95		
Shipping & handling: $3.50 per book		
Sales Tax (for MD residents only): $ .85 per book		
TOTAL:		

PAYMENT

☐ Check enclosed, made payable to BGCGW

☐ Visa   ☐ MasterCard   ☐ American Express

Card # _____

Expiration Date _____

Name as listed on card _____

Signature _____

SEND TO

Cookbook
Boys & Girls Clubs of Greater Washington
8555 16th Street, Suite 400
Silver Spring, MD 20910

For questions or quantity orders,
please call 301.562.2001.

For quantity discounts, call 301.562.2001 or email cookbook@bgcgw.org.

Photocopies will be accepted.

BOYS & GIRLS CLUBS
OF GREATER WASHINGTON